INDIANS IN TRANSITION

*A Study of Protestant Missions to Indians
in the United States*

by

G. E. E. LINDQUIST

*Field Representative of the Division of Home Missions, National Council
of Churches in the United States of America; Field Secretary
of the Society for Propagating the Gospel among the
Indians and Others in North America.*

With the Collaboration of

E. RUSSELL CARTER

Religious Work Director at Haskell Institute, Lawrence, Kansas

Foreword by

I. GEORGE NACE

*Executive Secretary, Division of Home Missions,
National Council of Churches of Christ in the U.S.A.*

87

Published by the

DIVISION OF HOME MISSIONS,
NATIONAL COUNCIL OF CHURCHES OF CHRIST IN THE U. S. A.

297 Fourth Avenue, New York 10, N. Y.

1951

The Allen Press
Lawrence, Kansas

DEDICATION

*To my co-workers in the Indian
Missionary Service covering a period
of forty fruitful years.*

CONTENTS

FOREWORD 9

INTRODUCTION 10

Part One:

FACTORS IN ECONOMIC AND SOCIAL ADJUSTMENT 13

   I. Population 13

  II. Social and Economic Conditions 14
      1. Percentage on relief
      2. Social and health problems due to poverty
      3. Social Security
      4. Employment
      5. Housing
      6. Native industries
      7. Leasing of land
      8. Commercial exploitation

 III. Social And Moral Conditions 18
      1. Use of alcohol
      2. Peyote
      3. Recreational activities
      4. Indian dances
      5. Civic, including wardship status
      6. Domestic
      7. Social feeling and public opinion
      8. Health and sanitation
      9. Educational
     10. Religious conditions, including hold of old religion

    Conclusions and Recommendations under Part I 27

Part Two:

**PRESENT STATUS AND EXTENT OF
PROTESTANT MISSIONARY WORK** 31

   I. Christian Agencies At Work 31
      1. Number
      2. Reservations and tribal groups
      3. Number of missions and projects

  II. Development of Native Leadership 33
      1. Development of native leadership
      2. Leadership training facilities
      3. Courses and institutes
      4. In-service training
      5. Furlough arrangements
      6. Personnel problems

III. **The Church** _____ **35**
  1. Equipment
  2. Membership and attendance
  3. Parish
  4. Sunday School
  5. Other Organizations
  6. Church Program
    a. Missionary
    b. Charitable and benevolent
    c. Industrial
    d. Civic
    e. Off the reservation
    f. Special work for young people
IV. **Program of Advance** _____ **40**
  1. Unreached fields
  2. Development needs
    a. Evangelistic work
    b. Educational
    c. Social
    d. Medical and other
V. **Chief Problems of Certain Areas** _____ **45**
  1. Southwest
  2. Plains
  3. How can Mission Boards help?
  4. The Church and Paternalism
  Conclusions and Recommendations under Part II ___ **48**
Part Three:

THE CHURCH AND THE INDIAN IN URBAN CENTERS ___ **54**
I. **The Urban Community Under Study** _____ **55**
  1. History of Indian-White Contact
II. **The Indian In Rapid City** _____ **56**
  1. Population and location
  2. Economic conditions
  3. Housing
  4. Attitudes
    a. Those of the Indian
    b. Community attitudes
III. **The Church and the Rapid City Indians** _____ **63**
  Conclusions and Recommendations under Part III **65**
  Appendix A. Phoenix Indian Service Center _____ **68**
  Appendix B. Questionnaire for City Pastors _____ **70**
  Appendix C. Questionnaire on Attitudes _____ **71**
Part Four:

SURVEY OF MISSION SCHOOLS _____ **72**
  1. Number and location
  2. Denominational affiliation
  3. History
  4. Organization
  5. Departments of instruction maintained
  6. Membership in state educational organizations

    7. Teaching staff
    8. Students
    9. Tribal representation
  10. Health
  11. Nearest Town
  12. Religious and Social Life
  13. Tuition
  14. Equipment and land
  15. Budget
  16. Program of Advance, with reference to future of mission
      schools.

Exhibit A. Federal Subsidies for Church-Operated Schools 77

Part Five:

**SURVEY OF ACTIVITIES OF RELIGIOUS WORK
DIRECTORS IN GOVERNMENT INDIAN SCHOOLS** **78**
  Schools Reporting
  Digest of Returns
 I. General Education Program **78**
    1. Age groups
    2. Tribes represented
    3. States represented
    4. Degree of Indian blood of students
    5. Cultural backgrounds
    6. Vocational emphasis
    7. Academic standards
    8. General objectives
 II. Religious Census _____ **80**
III. Program Of Religious Work Directors _____ **82**
    1. Length of service and experience
    2. Academic training
    3. Director's conception of his task
    4. Religious activities
    5. Student activities
    6. Future of schools
     **Appendix A. Report on Intermountain Indian
       School, Brigham City, Utah** _____ **86**
     **Appendix B. Report on Jones Academy,
       Hartshorne, Oklahoma** _____ **87**

Part Six:

PROTESTANT MISSIONS TO INDIANS IN U. S. A. _____ **88**

**Exhibit A. Listed by Regions, including denominations,
 tribes, locations** _____ **88**
Exhibit B. Some Overall Data _____ **98**
     I. Boards Constituent to the Division of Home Missions
       of the National Council of Churches of Christ in the
       U. S. A.
     II. Non-constituent or Non-sectarian
**Map of Cities Indicating Appreciable Indian Population;
 also Church Organizations at Work** _____**119**
Map of Indian Missionary Work in Oklahoma _____**120**

FOREWORD

In preparation for the National Congress on Home Missions, held at Columbus, Ohio, January 24-27, 1950, an Indian survey, intensive as well as comprehensive, was made. It was a project that required patient and painstaking labor.

Seeing its value to missionary workers as well as to all concerned and interested in the welfare of the American Indian, the seminar on Special Groups recommended that the survey be made available. This recommendation was unanimously approved by the Congress. The Executive Committee of the Home Missions Council of North America looked with favor upon the suggestion, and referred it to its Committee on Indian Work. In due time a sub-committee, consisting of Miss Katharine E. Gladfelter, Secretary of the Department of Educational and Medical Work, Board of National Missions of the Presbyterian Church in the United States of America; Miss Muriel Day, Executive Secretary, Bureau of Educational Institutions, Woman's Division of Christian Service of the Board of Missions and Church Extension of the Methodist Church; and Dr. Ross W. Sanderson, Director of Field Research of the Board of Home Missions of the Congregational and Christian Churches, was appointed to explore the possibility of having the study edited and printed. The members of the Committee, together with Miss Alice Maloney, Chairman of the Committee on Indian Work of the Division of Home Missions, National Council of Churches, have given valuable suggestions on the arrangement of material as well as reading the manuscript and offering helpful criticism.

We are especially indebted to Dr. G. E. E. Lindquist, who has given so many years of service to the Indians, and to Rev. E. Russell Carter, who was responsible for a section of the survey and who assisted in editing same.

This volume comes to you, not only for the factual information it contains, but also in the hope that it will inspire and stimulate its readers to participate more effectively in an intelligent approach to the problems which face the American Indian in his search for the more abundant life.

February, 1951

I. George Nace
Executive Secretary, Division of Home Missions, National Council of the Churches of Christ in the United States of America

INTRODUCTION

Since "Indians are people, are citizens and wage earners and property owners," is it not high time that "an intelligent and honorable program for bringing our Indian people into happy, respectable, self-supporting, full-fledged citizenship" be established? "Does our Government owe him _____ nan being than because he happens to bear the _____ he next steps?"

_____ seminar on the American Indians opened its _____ National Congress on Home Missions held at _____, Ohio, January, 1950. Just twenty years previously another Congress, the first of its kind, held at Washington, D.C., declared that "it is doubtful if any race has ever passed through such a succession of life-changing experiences as have the American Indians in the last 300 years. Throughout these years, the two most powerful influences in bringing Indians in contact with the white man's way of life have been the church and the government. Christian missionaries knew the Indian even before the government began its existence, and they have been reenforcing, supplementing and blazing new trails. The fact must be faced, however, that in spite of the efforts of government and church, great numbers of the Indians have remained indifferent and passive, clinging to as much of the old life as possible, adopting only such new ways as the fight for existence demanded. . . . The American Indians today are being plunged into still another transformation. The society of an industrial and machine age is closing in upon them and they are being forced increasingly to exert some effort in adjusting themselves to the prevailing civilization."[1]

That the process described above has been greatly intensified during the past two decades no one cognizant of Indian affairs can call into question. Today the Christian churches among our first Americans,—a title to which our Indians may properly lay claim,—confront an even greater challenge than in the past, making more urgent than before the need for united planning and action. Thus a study, such as the one presented in these pages, seemed appropriate and in keeping with the transition period through which Indian Americans are now passing.

Perhaps it is well to remind ourselves that the church has occupied an enviable place in the Indian country,—its influence far exceeding that of its numerical membership. The church has been and still is a pioneering agency. It pioneered in education and blazed new trails in the ministry of healing and mercy. Its emissaries represented peace rather than war and bloodshed. "When the Indians were without Christ it needed a standing army to control them,"—constitutes a well-attested fact as stated by a pioneer missionary. "The banks of the Missouri River (as well as oth-

---

[1] Report of Committee on Indians, Data Book, North American Home Missions Congress, Vol. 1, p. 49, December 1-5, 1930. Washington, D. C.

er streams and lakes) were dotted with military posts, and thousands of soldiers were stationed in these forts, well-armed with rifles, and ready at a moment's warning to go after hostile Indians who were committing severe depredations among the early settlers or upon other tribes. This has all passed away. Some of the forts remain in name only and serve as headquarters for Indian agencies and schools."[2]

The church has pioneered in bridging racial and tribal barriers. To-day native leaders are in charge of mission stations and hold pastorates among tribes other than their own. The old tribalism is passing. The church has lent its aid in the conservation and utilization of indigenous languages, in promoting literacy and putting heretofore unwritten languages into print. It has been a foremost factor in stabilizing community life though its unceasing emphasis on the monogamous family and responsibilities implicit in domestic relations.

Moreover, the church has conserved and developed the Indian's inherent religious impulse by making possible regular religious services in place of sporadic ceremonial observances characteristic of the old forms of worship. To consider adequately what is here involved would require a separate volume of its own. By training and using a native leadership it has sought to make the church indigenous to Indian life and thought.

In the field of experimentation the church has stressed new forms of social service. In many areas the church has served, and still does, as the natural community center. Thus it has increased its participation in issues having to do with economic justice as opposed to commercial exploitation. By stressing law and order, the exercise of citizenship rights, the conservation and utilization of the soil, the church has sought to make more effective the "Christian conscience" in twentieth century America.

While the number of church bodies ministering to Indians has increased and the amount of missionary money appropriated appears significant, there are factors which tend to temper any outbursts at self-congratulation. These will appear as the present study unfolds.

The purpose of the study may be stated as follows:
1. To secure up-to-date facts on Indians for use of Mission Boards and Agencies;
2. To furnish answers to questions which would, in turn, interpret the Indian work to church and constituency;
3. To affect procedures in the missionary program for the next decade.

In formulating plans for this evaluation the Committee on Survey suggested certain procedures, an important element of which was the gathering of data largely through a carefully prepared questionnaire. This, in turn, was sent to field workers, designated by their respective church

---

[2] "Twenty-five Years of the Association among the Sioux Indians" by Miss Mary Collins. Quoted from The American Missionary Magazine, 1907; published by the American Missionary Association, 287 Fourth Ave., N. Y.

officials, not only to those constituent to the Home Missions Council but to others as well.

Aside from the field questionnaire special studies have been made of (1) Indians in urban areas, (2) Mission Schools, (3) Religious Work Directors in Government Schools, and (4) an overall compilation covering certain aspects of Protestant Missions to Indians in the U. S. Under the latter is a listing both by states and sponsoring agencies of the Indian work being carried on in various regions.[3]

Rev. E. Russell Carter, Religious Work Director at Haskell Institute, Lawrence, Kansas, has given much time to gathering the data and formulating the report (Part Three) on Indians in urban and industrial centers. The schedules on Mission Schools as well as those of Religious Work Directors in Government Schools have been tabulated and summarized and are both incorporated as sections of this survey.

In tabulating the data from the field, the Indian country, for the sake of convenience, was divided into six areas, corresponding to the regional conference divisions of the National Fellowship of Indian Workers:

    I. Eastern—comprising New York and Michigan;
    II. Central or Plains—North and South Dakota, Nebraska, Iowa, Minnesota and Wisconsin;
    III. Pacific Northwest—Washington, Oregon, Idaho, and Montana;
    IV. Western—California, Nevada and Utah;
    V. Southwestern—North Mexico, Arizona and Colorado;
    VI. Oklahoma—Kansas, Oklahoma and Texas

Fifty-three questionnaires were turned in and the results of their tabulation largely furnish the basis for this report. While no survey of this nature can boast one hundred per cent or even seventy-five per cent returns, it is of interest to note that those submitted furnish a *representative sampling* both as to reservations (as well as areas where reservation conditions no longer prevail) and churches or agencies at work. In certain instances so called "spot studies" were made. Especially was this true of designated urban and industrial areas as well as of the work being carried on in government and mission schools.

---

[3] The work in Alaska is not included in this study.

PART ONE

Factors in Economic and Social Adjustment

Subjected to many changes in the past adaptability has ever marked Indian history as we know it. From the slow-moving Stone Age of pre-Columbian days to the high-powered industrial democracy of the present has demanded constant adjustment to changing conditions. That the transition period is still in process is evident today. Relocation as well as dislocation influence population trends. Intermarriage not only between Indians and non-Indians, but also intertribal, plays a prominent role in the assimilation process. Perhaps the most acute problems on the mission field today have to do not primarily with the general economic situation, serious as that is in certain areas, but rather with marriage and the home, the evils of peyote and the liquor traffic. Exposed to a century and a half of paternalism the blight of dependency and the lethargy of expectancy are factors to be reckoned with. This study indicates that some are content with the coveted status of incompetency while others clamor for full emancipation from governmental controls and a first-class citizenship.

As a part of this section consideration is also given to the present status with respect to superstition and custom, the influence of the tribal religious heritage, as well as certain psychological factors which could properly be conserved.

I. POPULATION

Designated as Indians and resident in the continental U.S. according to the Bureau of Indian Affairs are 393,622.[1] The U. S. Census of 1910 lists 265,683 with the explanatory note that "the Committee of Indian Affairs report 304,950 but this includes 25,927 freedmen and inter-married whites—among the Five Civilized Tribes—of Oklahoma." If, however, we accept the Bureau figures, it will be noted that the increase in Indian population has been 88,672 in 35 years. While much publicity has been given in recent years to the Navajo as the largest tribe numerically (61,000) and the one showing a rapid rate of increase more conservative reports indicate that the most marked increase for the Indian country as a whole has been among the mixed-bloods.

Commenting on the number of Indians not listed on tribal rolls nor enumerated as Indians, the Hoover Report states "the number is probably quite large but is not known." Perhaps the U. S. Census of 1950, when available, may throw some light on these. On the other hand, those on

---

[1] Statistical Supplement to the Annual Report of the Commissioner of Indian Affairs, 1945.

tribal rolls are often not resident on any reservation. This would apply to such states as Michigan, North Carolina, California, Oregon, Oklahoma, and to a certain degree in Wisconsin as pointed out herewith:

> "The Winnebago have no reservation in Wisconsin. They live in scattered localities and Indian communities in at least 19 counties in the state. There are a few families in Minnesota and Iowa. Principal settlements are near Black River Falls, Holmen, Wisconsin Dells and Wisconsin Rapids. Counties in which Winnebago reside are Adams, Chippewa, Clark, Columbia, Eau Claire, Green Lake, Jackson, Juneau, LaCrosse, Marathon, Monroe, Portage, Sauk, Shawano, Taylor, Trempealeau, Vernon, Waupaca and Wood. During the summer when following seasonal occupations they are scattered over even a wider area. The total Winnebago population according to Indian Bureau statistics is 1520."

Included among population factors is intermarriage, not only as between Indians and non-Indians, but intertribal as well. The past 25 years have witnessed an increase in both. Whereas intermarriage between certain tribes and non-Indians was almost unknown 25 years ago it is now fairly common and on the increase. Intertribal marriages are also on the increase due, in part, to the influence of non-reservation schools such as Haskell, and contacts established in off-the-reservation employment and residence.

The opening paragraphs of the Hoover Committee Report on Indian Affairs show a grasp of the bearing on these population changes, refreshingly free from any romanticism which would seek to maintain the status quo of pre-Columbian days in a twentieth century setting:

> "Indians are people. Indians are citizens. Indians are wage earners and salaried employees. Indians are ranchers, farmers, and businessmen. Indians are property owners. Such obvious facts are so often overlooked that it is desirable to begin any discussion of Indian affairs by calling them to mind.
>
> "In most parts of the country, nearly everywhere except the Southwest and Alaska, *the 'Indian' of popular imagination has all but vanished. The Indian lives much as other men in his region do and makes his living in the same ways.* He is of mixed bloods—as are other Americans. He dresses, speaks, looks, and acts very much like his neighbors. He has the same problems, plus others of his own that are the product of his past and of present circumstances. There is in every tribe, however, a group of 'full bloods' who continue some of the tribal customs, speak the tribal language, and perhaps wear some articles of Indian dress, frequently moccasins. Outside of the Southwest and Alaska they are usually a minority varying in size from tribe to tribe, but probably less than *twenty-five percent in many. Although referred to as 'full bloods,' many so-called have some non-Indian blood, and some men of exclusively Indian blood are not thought of as being in the 'full blood' group.*"[2]

II. SOCIAL AND ECONOMIC STATUS

1. Relief

While the general economic situation is acute on many reservations the percentage of the Indian population receiving relief is appreciably lower than 10 years ago. At that time the largest number on relief was from the Plains Region with 87%, the smallest from the Southwest with

---

[2] Quoted from: Report of the Committee on Indian Affairs to the Commission on Organization of the Executive Branch of the Government, October, 1948, p. 1.

21%. However, largely reflected on the Navajo and Hopi reservations, relief figures have taken a decided jump in that area within recent years; extracts from the American Red Cross indicate:

"More than half the Navajo families in this area were in need of assistance.

"Of the 2,002 families given food orders, approximately 75 percent had not previously been on the welfare rolls of the Navajo and Hopi Agencies. . .

"48.6 percent of these families had health problems, involving one or more members, that were obvious to the layman. . .

"In 57.8 percent of the families there were employable males, but no opportunities for employment were available to them on the reservation and no employment outside the reservation would be available until the late spring and summer months."[2a]

2. Poverty and Contributing Causes

A Navajo worker sums up the social and health problems due to poverty and other contributing causes briefly and succinctly:

"The high incidence of tuberculosis, and some undernourishment, may be traced to poverty. Poverty is not the only factor, however; ignorance of the need for sanitation and protection against infection by tubercular patients, reliance upon the superstitious practices and teachings of the medicine-men are responsible for much of our trouble.

"Some of the undernourishment results from misuse of the earnings and resources of the parents responsible for children. Liquor, peyote, automobiles and gasoline, sometimes receive what should have gone for food and clothing for the children.

"A serious social problem results from the separation of families as men go out to work on railroad jobs in distant states. Young girls away from parental supervision and guidance while at work in towns and cities, have frequently made undesirable marriages or they become involved in unhappy relationships, not to mention worse problems."

3. Social Security

Since all Indians, with the exception of those in New Mexico and Arizona,[3] may avail themselves of social security for the aged, the blind and dependent children; the issuing of rations, so common in earlier decades, shows a marked decrease.

At the National Fellowship of Indian Workers Conference, held at Bacone College, Bacone, Oklahoma, June, 1949, the seminar on the Indian study reports:

"Social and health problems (in connection with poverty and relief) are largely due to a 'parasitic philosophy.' Paternalism provides for the moment, but is morally destructive. Unless handled carefully rummage sales may do harm to givers and receivers alike if allowed to become a major part of the mission program."

4. On and Off the Reservation Employment

In the Navajo country the total labor supply available during the summer is 14,600. A director and assistants for on and off reservation jobs are in charge of carrying this forward.

In the West and Pacific Northwest migrant jobs such as fruit pick-

---

[2a] Released from Red Cross Headquarters, 1949.

[3] In the spring of 1950 arrangements were made whereby the states took over the administration of assistance grants, under a plan approved by the Federal Security Agency. The Government pays up to 92 per cent of the grants. At first only 65 per cent of the Navajo's budgetary needs was met, but since Sept. 1950, full payments have been made each month. For example, in October 1950 $15,720.34 was paid to 359 Navajo families on the reservation as a whole.—From News Release of Dec. 29, 1950, Window Rock, Ariz.

ing, hops picking, etc., are available; also work in lumber mills, day laborers on ranches, etc. In the Eastern area many work in plants off the reservation, for example near Niagara Falls and Buffalo; here also construction workers in steel, e. g. bridge builders, find a labor market. A number were employed on the new United Nations buildings in New York City.

At the present time, except in the more isolated areas, Indians may secure employment under state or federal agencies.

5. Housing

An encouraging element in the housing situation as compared to 10 years ago is the desire for improvement. However, off-the-reservation living conditions, as noted in the special report on Indians in urban centers, do not tend to foster morality; overcrowding and slum conditions are the rule rather than the exception in altogether too many industrial areas where Indians reside.

A few specific instances are cited herewith—one from the Pacific Northwest, one each from the Plains and Lakes Region, while still another from California, coupled with two or three samples from the Southwest. Neah Bay, Washington, reports progress in housing:

> "During the War a large construction project was located on the reservation, and since that time the tribe has purchased all the buildings left by that camp. There were roughly 15 small 3 room dwellings, 24 - 30 medium 5 room dwellings, and about 10 duplex apartments which have been converted into 5 and 6 room homes. These buildings were moved into the village proper, remodeled, and resold to individuals upon easy terms.
>
> "This project, along with the other modest but adequate homes, have virtually eliminated the old unsatisfactory dwellings in the town. There are few families who do not have adequate, if not pretentious, housing. There is still some overcrowding due to large families, and also due to slowness of furnishings and arranging the houses they have. In these cases one might say that immorality is fostered because of crowding and the lack of privacy, but on the whole, the present housing tends more to be normal for a small medium prosperous community than otherwise."

From Rosebud, South Dakota, comes a less favorable report:

> "The present housing situation is very bad. During 1938 a few houses in about 4 communities were built with rehabilitation funds. During 1939-40 the Government offered $100 for hardware, windows, roof, etc., to any Indian who would haul the logs and do the rest of the building. The Rosebud Agency has for a number of years advocated a LONG RANGE HOUSING PROGRAM, but has been unable to get the necessary appropriation from Congress. Supt. Whitlock says that this has been approved by the Indian Office. The plan is this: To spend $12,000 a year for 10 years. This would be a self-help program similar to the one used in 1939-40. The Government would undertake to provide the hardware, windows, roof, etc., for a one room house. If the person for whom the house was to be built wanted any additional rooms, he could pay for them at the rate of $200 for each additional room. The Government would make loans for the purpose. The principle behind this plan is to help the Indian help himself."

From White Earth, Minnesota:

> "The housing conditions are better than in some areas due to the building of a number of small houses by WPA projects which rent to the Indians for a very small amount. There are not enough of these to meet the demand, and in some cases ten to fifteen people including several families are living in one house. These conditions foster a great deal of immorality and indifference to the most simple decencies of life.

16

There are continual reports of incest, the latest of which is the rape of a 10 year old stepdaughter by the stepfather."

Bishop, California, reports "two-thirds in Government built houses and one-third in cabins;" Livingston, Texas, "Most houses too small, new ones being built." Less encouraging is that of the Ute Mountain area (Colorado) : "Live in tents and hogans; a few in one room houses. No tendency to better conditions." At Yuma, Arizona, "All live in stick and adobe houses; destroyed when death occurs;" Zuni, New Mexico, "Better off in housing; some building homes away from the pueblo."

6. Native Industries

a. BASKETRY AND BEAD-WORK, once quite general among Indian tribes, are reported as disappearing. In the Southwest rug weaving, pottery, silver-smithing are still factors. Indian Wells, Navajo, reports, "One-half of the living comes from rug weaving." In certain other tourist areas an effort is being made to promote native crafts with indifferent results. In Oklahoma the Mohonk Lodge and the Sequoyah Weavers have made commendable progress in encouraging these industries.

b. ANY INDIAN CO-OPS? The answer is that there are a number. One sponsored by missionary agencies is of special interest and indicative of what may be done in other areas:

"Among the Winnebago native industries basketry and beadwork are an important source of income. Sponsored by the Evangelical and Reformed Church Mission a *cooperative organization, The Winnebago Handcraft Cooperative, was formed and incorporated under the laws of the state of Wisconsin* to find a wider market for their handicraft. Monthly meetings of members are held at the Mission recreation hall at the Black River Falls settlement. Out of savings a small cooperative grocery store was begun which is serving the community. During periods of unemployment the Indians can trade handicraft at standard prices for groceries. Part of this handicraft is shipped to distant markets and part of it is stored for resale to members for their roadside stands during the tourist season.

"Since its establishment the cash income from handicraft annually sold through the Cooperative is as follows: 1941—$377.00; 1942—$1,112.00; 1943—$6,178.00; 1944—$5,743.00; 1945—$11,413.00; 1946—$21,887.00; 1947—$3,954.00; 1948—$4,212.00."

7. Leasing of Land

According to the Statistical Supplement of 1945 the amount of "non-Indian operated" land, including tribal and trust allotted but not Government owned, amounted to the staggering total of 31,158,443 acres.

In the Southwest, Pima reports, "Irrigated land to both Indians and whites; e. g. 90% in Salt River area; 10 to 20% at Gila River." In the Northwest, Yakima, Washington, "Of 1,126,554 acres, 406,635 are leased to Indians for grazing; 13,500 acres for farming." In western Oklahoma where the leasing evil has been a major problem for years the Kiowa Agency reports 409,109 acres leased to non-Indians.

Commenting on the general leasing situation the Hoover Committee pointedly remarks:

"It is of greatest importance that Indian owners be encouraged, aided, and stimulated in every way to use their own resources, chiefly land, wherever practicable. The more that is known of Indian affairs, past and present, the clearer becomes the wisdom of this policy. The benefit to the Indian is two-fold. He increases his income, and he acquires that experience as a farmer or rancher or business man that is indispensable to true 'competence.' There is a world of experience to show that Indian

17

owners increase their income when they stop leasing their lands to others and put them to use themselves. Successful experience of this sort is also of enormous benefit in maturing Indians in the values of modern economic life. They know what 'capital' means. They do not dissipate their assets. *They hold on to their land; and they pay their debts.*"[4]

8. Commercial Exploitation

Do Indians suffer from commercial exploitation? The answers vary from "extreme" in the Osage county (Oklahoma) to "Indians so poor, not worthwhile" in the flint hills and scrub oak country of old Indian Territory. Several mention "high price of food in local stores (traders);" "take advantage of Indian low sales resistance;" another, "Pendleton (Oregon) round-up hires Indians to appear in exhibitions, encourages old time and heathenish customs, definitely an unfavorable practice for Indians as a whole;" another Westerner says, "favored as much as whites or even more." The majority indicate "not to a marked extent" and "not as much as formerly."

III. SOCIAL AND MORAL CONDITIONS

1. Use of Alcohol

a. No one cognizant of Indian life and affairs within the past decade can escape the conviction that the use of alcoholic beverages has greatly increased. In the Southwest all except one speak of "a tremendous increase, extensive boot-legging and little attempt to enforce laws;" some refer to it as "the greatest evil," "worse than pre-war;" "worst in the history of the reservation." However, in two areas "a slight decrease since the war" is noted; another says "ten per cent give us all the trouble."

b. ATTITUDE TOWARD REPEAL. The opinion is divided. Typical comments are, "the better class Indians are opposed;" "repeal means equalization before the law;" "generally under certain conditions off-the-reservation;" "ex-servicemen and workers off-the-reservation don't like the discrimination (of special liquor laws); "and want it like white men." On the other hand "the older ones are opposed to repeal."

The Hoover Report has much to say on "The Indian Liquor Law" and its repeal, part of which is quoted herewith:

> "The immediate effect of repeal may be to increase drinking for a time, as did the end of national prohibition. If so, it is believed that the increase would not last. Whether there is a long run increase in drinking among Indians will depend upon other forces, e. g., their general economic position, the handling of destitution, the maintenance of law and order, and the attainment of a more satisfactory way of living generally. Despite the almost universal resentment of the Indian liquor law by Indians, they are well aware of the evil of drunkenness and are frank to admit it is a problem. In this respect they are perhaps more realistic than many white communities. Drunkenness should be dealt with and the law against drunken and disorderly conduct should be enforced. It is believed that tribal authorities will not be inclined to change their policy on this point.
>
> "Until responsibility for law and order on a reservation has passed to the state, there should be tribal 'local option' on the question of selling liquor on the reservation. If permitted, the sale should be regulated as nearly as possible in accordance with the method prevailing in the state."

---

[4] Op. Cit., p. 80.

2. Peyote

In the Southwest, especially among the Navajos, the use of peyote is "increasing;" however, "while its use has become much more widespread" during the past ten years, "in some areas, a lessening use, due to cases of insanity and some instances of sudden death, attributed to peyote, has frightened some." Utes (Colorado) "A greater number favor peyote and believe it has all power to heal sickness and save their souls."

In Oklahoma, on the other hand, some report "a decrease" or "remaining stationary." In the Dakotas "its use is concentrated in certain communities" while in the Pacific Northwest it is "still unheard of" for the most part.

In spite of the alarming use of peyote in many areas of the Indian country it is passing strange that the Hoover Committee on Indian Affairs has no word, much less recommendation, on this social evil. Nor has any recent Commissioner of Indian Affairs taken any positive stand since Mr. John Collier condoned its use on the ground that peyote was a sacramental substance like the bread and wine of the communion services.[5] However, "on November 26, 1948, the Secretary of the Interior released a report by a committee of prominent doctors appointed by the American Medical Association . . . which described peyote as a habit-forming drug which acts on the nervous system as a stimulant and narcotic and recommended that Congress pass a law to restrict the sale and possession of peyote." This is quoted from "Your Religion" by Superintendent H. E. Bruce of the Winnebago Agency, Nebraska, who also states that "90% of the Omaha and over 50% of the Winnebago Indians" are addicted to its use.[6]

3. Recreational Activities

a. TYPES: Under this heading are tribal dances, sports, rodeos, fiestas, gambling, horse races, games, parties, movies, scouting; also cited, "Bingo at the Roman Catholic Church." Where missions have parish and community halls they take the initiative in providing organized recreational activities. For the most part the schools are active, especially mission schools.

4. Indian Dances

Indian dances, such as "ceremonial stomp dances," squaw dances, sun dances, etc., are held seasonally, "mostly during summer" or "quarterly" or "once a year." Some report "not as many as formerly," or "pretty much a thing of the past." In the Southwest thirteen say "they are very prevalent."

Among effects, direct or indirect, are listed: "Large percentage kept in old superstitions and progress retarded," "lack of home responsibility, leave sheep and children alone," "loose morals—jealousy, drinking, gambling," "stealing and fighting," "absenteeism of school children," "men lose working time." Several, however, report "some value for social life."

---

[5] See Hearings on Interior Department Appropriation Bill for 1936, p. 690.

[6] Report released April 12, 1949 and printed in News Letter of the National Fellowship of Indian Workers No. 40, Autumn, 1949.

5. Civic

a. INFLUENCE OF TRIBAL COURTS

Reports vary from "pretty good" to "fair," "weak," "completely nil" to "corrupt;" four report "influence for good but effect limited as they have control over minor misdemeanors only." From the Navajo:

> "Undoubtedly the tribal courts have some beneficial effect, serving as a deterrent in some measure. However, there is lack of law enforcement. We have a set of law and order regulations and native courts for the trial of cases brought before them. Sentences are light, and many think it no disgrace to serve a sentence in jail. During recent years it has become a commonplace for a prisoner to send word that he needs help and relatives collect among themselves and from friends sufficient money to pay a fine, and the prisoner goes out without stigma or obligation. Many policemen have but scant knowledge of the law and order regulations."[7]

b. STATE JURISDICTION

is advocated by a vast majority where such is not already the case, especially with respect to marriage and divorce. Among reasons given are: "Marriage relation would be stronger and more meaningful," "would stabilize home life," "make Indians more acceptable and responsible citizens," "would hasten the assimilation process." Those registering disapproval say, "State is like the Indian Bureau in Washington" and "Indian doesn't get a square deal in state courts; smart lawyers may impose on him."

c. SUFFRAGE. *Do Indians vote?*

In Michigan Indians have voted since 1856 and in New York since 1924; in New Mexico and Arizona some voted for the first time in the last presidential election (1948). In Oklahoma all say "Yes," except where "many refuse to vote" (Kickapoo). In Montana one reports "all vote but only a few can do their own leasing;" in one or two states "a literacy test" is mentioned as a deterrent.

d. WARDSHIP.

(1) *What is Indian reaction to wardship?* From the Southwest: "Older ones want it, younger ones don't," "most deplore it but hesitate to assume responsibilities of full citizenship;" some say "fifty-fifty" or "opinion divided;" others, "have had a taste of freedom, only those who don't want responsibility want wardship;" "matter of expediency, useful for personal gain." In other sections, for example central Oklahoma, "wardship is limited to trust lands and accounts in excess of $500 to $1000 — the latter varying according to tribe."

(2) *Non-Indian reaction:* "Attitude of condescension in dealing with Indians; latter dubbed inferior for not bearing share of taxation;" "most white people would like to see Indians denounce wardship." From the Puget Sound comes a statement reflecting a superiority complex all too prevalent:

> "The non-Indian portion of the population is for the most part resentful of, and considers itself much superior to, the Indian. The general opinion seems to be that 'the Indian has gotten all that is coming to him,' and also that he has many advantages that he does not deserve. I believe that the attitude would be that he should receive no more assistance from the government; whether these same people would be in favor of placing the Indian beyond governmental supervision, I'm not so sure."

---

[7] According to Circuit Court Judge Turner M. Rudesill, "Tribal courts have no authority whatsoever to set up courts and furthermore, they are wholly illegal." Rapid City, South Dakota Journal, August 21, 1950.

Here is another slant, this time from Wisconsin, but by no means confined to that state:

"The whole matter of wardship is hardly given a thought by white people. *Ignorance concerning Indian affairs and the Indians' status is appalling.* Most white people even those who should know better have a vague opinion that all Indians are somehow supported by the Government and it comes somewhat as a surprise when they hear that an Indian in order to live must work for a living the same as a white man. *Of course, they are opposed to a termination of wardship of the Indian if it means that the Indian would then become a responsibility entirely of the locality in which he happens to live. Much education both of the Indian and the white man regarding the whole idea of wardship* is needed before either Indian or white can arrive at a reasoned opinion in the matter."

In concluding this section a paragraph is quoted from the "General Recommendations" of the Hoover Committee Report, which while it does not mention wardship by that name does emphasize the importance of *"target dates"* in the "progressive transfer to state and local governments" of functions now exercised by the Indian Bureau:

"Action should be scheduled and target dates fixed for each important step in the completion of the program. Time schedules are of benefit to the President and Congress in making overall financial plans. They are useful for the Bureau of Indian Affairs in administering the broad program. But they are indispensable for the Indian people themselves. There is a great deal of difference between preparing for an uncertain even though expected event and preparing for an event on a determined date. Indian leaders need this certainty in working with their own people. A great deal of discussion by Indian people will be necessary in preparing themselves for additional responsibilities. Fixed dates will be useful in pointing up the thinking and in stimulating realism in facing their economic problems."[8]

6. Domestic

a. THE MARRIAGE SITUATION

While it is noted that Indian custom marriages register a decline as compared to ten years ago, it is also a fact that the reverse is true in some instances; two areas in the Western region report "a great deal of common law" and in the Southwest (Hopi) "large majority old Indian way." In Oklahoma "some common law later consummated by legal rites." It may come as a surprise to learn that Oklahoma still countenances common law marriages.

A disquieting report from Wisconsin which also indicates a trend is quoted herewith:

"The marriage situation is deplorable. From 1919 to 1923 noble and successful efforts were made by the superintendents of the Winnebago agency to bring Winnebago under the state laws regulating domestic relationships. After 1932 the whole program was thrown overboard with disastrous results. Young people came to believe it was a disgrace for an Indian to allow himself to be bound by the white man's laws. The powers that be accepted any kind of, even the loosest, relationship between men and women as 'Indian custom marriage.' Divorce was just as easy and as common. During the years before World War II legal marriage was almost unknown. Gradually now the consciousness is dawning that an appellation of 'Indian custom' to any kind of the loosest marriage relationship is actually a term of disrespect and disgrace toward the Indian. There are no actual statistics of marriage and divorce available either at the agency office or elsewhere because of the situation (non-reservation) of the Winnebago."

---

[8] Op. cit., p. 76.

b. To the question, *"Are Indians encouraged by the responsible authorities to be legally married?"* a more encouraging response by far than ten years ago is noted. In the Southwest all but two say "Yes;" the same is true in the Pacific Northwest and Central regions. One says, however, "Question is pretty much ignored."

c. Associated with the *instability of the marital relation* are promiscuity, separations, divorces and broken homes. In the more primitive areas promiscuity looms large though divorces are "little known;" in less isolated areas the way to the white man's divorce court has been discovered, where it is said "a large number divorce first spouse;" others say "divorces (or separations) not permanent," or "same as among whites."

7. Social Feeling and Public Opinion

a. ANY RACE PREJUDICE BETWEEN INDIANS AND NON-INDIANS?

This varies somewhat according to geography, backgrounds and cultural contacts. In Oklahoma "very little" or "not noticeable" or "not more than between rich and poor," that is, social rather than racial. In the far West one records "prejudice between Indians and Mexicans;" in the central region "between mixed-bloods and full-bloods" in certain localities; also one comments, "Indians make their own barriers," that is "some Indians segregate themselves." In Montana "white residents object to Indian children in public schools." The latter is not nearly as common as ten or fifteen years ago.[9]

b. THE CHURCH AND SCHOOL (including government, mission and public) are generally reported as *the two most influential factors directing public opinion;* however, in the Southwest, nine list "old Indian religion" or the "peyote cult" ahead of both church and school.

c. IS RELIGIOUS DENOMINATIONALISM STRONG? Generally speaking not, except in certain "hot spots." Some are happy to record that "it has never been stressed." Another report states: "While religious denominationalism is strong (especially between Protestants and Roman Catholics) there is an element of friendliness and cooperation between the two churches which seems to be widespread and not present on any other reservation that I know of." Another reports "much drifting from one denomination to another" — in other words, instances of "interlocking church memberships."

d. DO INDIANS BELONG TO CIVIC CLUBS? Yes, in a number of instances, especially in Oklahoma. In the Western region some belong to "almond growers association;" "participate in athletics and singing conventions;" in Michigan some are Masons, the latter being true in the Southwest where "a few native professional people in the Government service, especially from other tribes, belong to the Masons and other fraternal organizations."

e. IS THE ATTITUDE OF THE WHITE COMMUNITY (where dominant) one of exclusion, or ignoring of Indians in civic and social affairs, or *one of inviting participation?* In very few instances are there evidences of outright exclusion. However, four check this in the Pacific Northwest with

---

[9] See also *"Indians in Urban Centers"* by G. E. E. Lindquist, 7 Winona Street, Lawrence, Kansas, 1948.

the comment that "the whites are critical in their attitudes;" the majority indicate that of "inviting participation," though in some cases there is the qualifying phrase "inviting participation to those who keep standards high." In Michigan the report states that "Indians are not ignored in social affairs." At the Bacone Conference the seminar group opinion as recorded revealed:

> "Indians take part in certain civic organizations but they are generally ignored. Certain exceptions show happy mingling in civic and social affairs."

8. Health and Sanitation

a. DISEASE. That tuberculosis still is number one killer in certain areas is intimated, e. g. Navajo, "fourteen to one as compared to the white population" while Yuma (Arizona) reports "average much lower than in the white world;" in the Pacific Northwest five say "very few cases;" Oklahoma, "eight times that of general population." From the Plains region, Rosebud, South Dakota:

> "Tuberculosis is very prevalent. Out of 1108 admissions to the Rosebud Hospital in 1948, 29 or .026% were for tuberculosis, but this is by no means representative of the general situation. It is hard to get the people to come in for that because so many have waited too long and have died in hospitals and sanitoria. Trachoma is disappearing on this reservation because the health department has been warring on it for many years, and through its school examinations has been able to find and treat all cases among school children. In spite of the large proportion found and treated only 72 cases or .065% of the 1948 admissions were for trachoma. Venereal disease is one of the worst health problems, having reached epidemic proportions. There were 50 or .046% admissions in 1948. During 1949 with the vigilant cooperation of the police department the number of admissions has increased tremendously."

Brief but pertinent comment with respect to trachoma and venereal diseases: From the Navajo: "In twenty years trachoma has become a minor problem; venereal disease more apparent now because of better records;" Eastern: trachoma, none; venereal disease: "About the same as whites."

b. HOSPITAL FACILITIES are for the most part under Government auspices "for Indians" although in the far West and certain of the Plains states county and community hospitals are available on an interracial basis. In the Southwest mission hospitals and clinics have played a significant role in the ministry of healing and still function to full capacity. At Ganado Mission, Arizona, a training school for Indian nurses under efficient church leadership has been in operation for about fifteen years.

c. That AN ADEQUATE PROGRAM OF HEALTH PROTECTION and medical treatment is essential in any civilized community today and especially in the assimilation stage all will agree. The Hoover Committee recommends that "responsibility for public health functions should be transferred to state and local governments wherever possible."

> "Using the local public health organizations will help Indians to orient themselves toward their state and local governments instead of looking to 'Uncle Sam' for everything; it will help to break down barriers between Indian and white communities, and it will be dealing with health as a health problem, which it is, rather than as an Indian problem.
> "In the meantime while medical care is being provided by Indian Service staff physicians, a schedule of fees for medical treatment should

23

be established by the Bureau of Indian Affairs, and fees should be collected from all Indians who are able to pay."

9. Educational

a. Twenty-five years ago any educational survey would note the passing of Protestant Mission Schools; fifteen years ago marked *the passing of a number of Government Schools,* not only on the reservations but also the non-reservation type. Today one may comment on the emergence of the public schools as the medium of educating Indian children; and in practically all areas they are open to their admission. In fact, the preponderance of Government schools is confined largely to the Southwest.

b. INADEQUATE SCHOOL FACILITIES are also largely confined to the Southwest — more especially the Navajo where estimates vary from 14,000 to 16,000 with respect to children "out of school." Just to cite one example — "In the Chinle school district there are 4,600 of which only 700 are in school, either Government or Mission." In that area the mission schools are still greatly in demand "and would best serve our needs," as voiced by the field workers and their Indian constituents.

c. The percentage of ADULT ILLITERACY is also high in the Navajo area, one report placing the figure at 41,000. In all other areas the percentage of illiteracy has decreased in recent decades. Where school attendance is enforced illiteracy is rapidly on the wane. Even in isolated areas "Indians are slowly learning the value of an education;" then too, "men in the armed services have attended school." Another says "Old die, youth attend schools." In certain communities, especially noted in eastern Oklahoma "Indians are more literate than white." In Texas "due to the closing of segregated reservation schools and more opportunities offered in public schools there is hope for college training."

d. Everywhere in the Indian country today there is not only the desire on the part of parents that their children should avail themselves of existing educational facilities but *more interest in better schools* and better trained teachers with an enriched curriculum. The need for the latter is voiced in a report from White Earth, Minnesota:

> "The educational problem of the Indians in this community is not one of adequate number of schools or facilities, but of a system of teaching the Indian children those things which will prepare them to provide themselves and their families with a living in society. When they emerge from school either after finishing the eighth grade, and a year or two of high school, or when they are 16 years old and have sometimes completed satisfactorily only a few grades, they are utterly unprepared to do anything which will earn for themselves or a family a living. They are unskilled and unable to compete with the lowest paid type of common labor; so have no alternative but to continue to maintain a bare existence in those communities where there is no hope or opportunity of any kind. Eventually they become delinquents in every sense of the word."

The Bacone Conference took cognizance of this educational lag as well as the desirability for vocational training and plans for providing scholarships. The resolutions dealing with this are worthy of serious consideration.[10]

---

[10] See Fellowship News Letter No. 39, Summer edition, 1949; also p. 128 ff. of the Hoover Committee Report.

10. General Religious Conditions

a. SUPERSTITION AND CUSTOMS — How firm a hold?

In the Southwest thirteen (out of 16 reporting) say "very strong;" on the other hand, three reply "very little" or "in some cases." From Papago:

> "Quite strong among older people, who often have influence at home over children and grandchildren. Percentage hard to estimate, because hidden from non-Indians as being uncivilized. Believe it to be decreasing as education progresses."

In the Pacific Northwest the "hold" is definitely diminishing. One puts it this way: "Little more than with comparable economic and social class of white people." In fact, every area reports "a steady decrease," with "very little" persecution or ostracism visited on those who "break away," that is "if they really show the determination to break away;" "sometimes ostracism but no persecution." Reasons given are: "Influence of Christian teaching and education," "changing civilization," "contact with other tribes as well as with non-Indians."

b. OLD RELIGION

Considered under this heading are: influence of "medicine men;" influence of tribal heritage in relation to Christian profession; at what points old religion and Christianity are similar.

From the Papago country in Arizona:

> "Hard to tell since Catholicism was introduced around 1700. Aboriginal celebrations appear to have been turned into Saint's Days. Influence of medicine men generally decreasing, amount of decrease depending upon adequate medical coverage of reservation. Native religion has been merged with Christianity for centuries."

Elsewhere in the Southwest: "Only form, no meaning;" medicine men losing out due to mission hospitals and preaching." In Texas: "They were moon worshippers once but this superceded by Christianity. . ." "Chief says he's never seen any medicine men here." From Oklahoma: "Youth don't understand and are not interested." In at least one New York reservation (Tuscarora): "No long house or pagan Indians here."

Perhaps it should be noted also that "systematic worship distinguishes Christianity as contrasted with non-Christian religions," especially those practiced by Indians of the plains or buffalo-hunting areas. In the far West one report says, "Indian religion similar to certain parts of the Old Testament; both have record of flood, both looking for coming of Son of Man; both emphasize sacrifice; moral laws rigidly kept and given them by an angel of God."

Of special significance is this statement from Wisconsin, revealing unusual insights and characteristic of other areas in the Plains region:

> "Perhaps a third of the Winnebago still adhere in some measure to the old religion. The power of the 'medicine' man has declined. The white man's medicine, modern education, the church and the peyote cult are some of the causes favoring this trend. Christianity does have a great attraction for the Winnebago. Its outlook on life, its liberating power from fear of spirits, its teaching of the love of God for man, the sacrifice on the Cross for man's salvation and the promise of an abiding companion Spirit have a powerful appeal to the Winnebago mind. But so too have some of the elements of the old Indian cult, the idea of guardian spirits; visions, as glimpses into the mysterious hidden world; outward and visible means of obtaining blessings and making con-

25

tact with the realm of the spirits (medicines, offerings of tobacco, moccasins, deerskins, rattles, tom-toms, fetishes, charms, etc.); the social aspects of religious ceremonies and observances, etc. No doubt the great attraction of the Peyote cult has been in its ability to combine these elements of Christianity and paganism so the Indian could have both.

"For the Winnebago every aspect of life is religious and religion is life. It is impossible to divorce life from religion. During every fleeting moment the quality of daily existence is contingent upon the will of the spirits. Man's dependency is absolute. This awareness of the divine presence is a religious value that might well be carried over. Another is his deep sense of wonder and reverence. Also worthy of carrying over are something of the social aspects of his religious observances and his generosity."

CONCLUSIONS AND RECOMMENDATIONS[11]
PART ONE

1. Population Factors

a. *Mobility* rather than stability is indicative of present trends; those on tribal rolls are often not resident on any reservation, e.g. states like New York, Michigan, Wisconsin, California, Oregon and Oklahoma.

b. *Presence of mixed-bloods* in increasing numbers constitutes another population factor. Approximately two-thirds of individuals arbitrarily classified as "Indians" on the government rolls are of mixed ancestry. Thus the Indian of popular imagination has all but vanished. It is high time to cease to think of the Indian as being different, rather should one consider his essential humanity. Our government, as well as our churches, owe him more because he is a human being than because he happens to bear the name of "Indian."

2. Social and Economic Status

a. *Relief.* The percentage of Indian population receiving relief is appreciably lower than it was ten years ago except among Navajos. Social and health problems (in connection with poverty and relief) may in certain cases be due to high incidences of tuberculosis, undernourishment, separation of families in off-the-reservation employment, as well as paternalistic attitudes.

b. *Housing.* An encouraging element in the housing situation is the desire for improvement; however, off-the-reservation living conditions (see Part Three) do not tend to foster morality; overcrowding and slum conditions are the rule rather than the exception in altogether too many industrial areas where Indians reside.

c. *Employment opportunities* for Indians, both on and off the reservations, should be encouraged. Cooperation with resettlement projects, sponsored by governmental agencies, such as proposed for the Southwest and Northern Plains states, is urged.

d. *Native industries,* as such, seem to be on the wane, while handicrafts, such as basketry and weaving are on the increase, especially in tourist areas. Experiments in Indian cooperative ventures are going forward but only to a limited extent.

e. *Leasing* of land to non-Indians is still a vexing problem, although

---

11 Some of these recommendations were submitted to the Indian Section of the National Congress on Home Missions, held at Columbus, Ohio, January 1950. Not only did they furnish a basis for discussion but a number were embodied in the Findings of that historic meeting. See *"For A Christian World"*, pp. 49-51. Published by Home Missions Division, National Council of Churches, New York.

At the request of the Committee on Survey the Bacone Conference of the National Fellowship of Indian Workers, held at Bacone College, Oklahoma, June 1949, was asked to consider certain proposals growing out of this study as well as bring in concrete recommendations. Some of these are also incorporated herewith.

Government authorities and tribal business committees are encouraging the use of the Indian's own resources which usually is *land*.

f. *Commercial* exploitation is not as prevalent as formerly.

g. *Liquor*. Liquor seems to hold a firm place as "public enemy number one;" moreover, the use of alcoholic beverages is on the increase. With respect to repeal of existing liquor laws the opinion is divided; the "better class" Indians are opposed; on the other hand ex-service men and workers off-the-reservation don't like the discrimination, "want it like white men."

In recent years several regional conferences of Indian workers have recorded their "disapproval of the movement to make liquor available legally because the Indian is particularly susceptible to the effects of liquor and easily becomes demoralized and degraded from its use."

The Christian standard is that human relations are a much deeper matter than law, that the kingdom to be conquered, the battle to be fought is in the mind and heart of man. In short, human nature must be changed.

h. *Peyote and Drug Addiction*.

Inasmuch as peyote continues to be a menace to the Indians whether used as a drug or a cult, we urge:

(1) That aggressive action toward prohibiting the traffic in peyote through legislative action be continued;

(2) Inasmuch as the available supply of literature on peyote is meagre and the supply practically exhausted, be it resolved that we call on the Home Mission Boards and agencies, as well as the Home Missions Division of the National Council, to supply reprints of such literature which has continuing value; that suitable tracts be prepared which might have wide distribution, giving, for example, the testimonies of former Peyote users as well as other pertinent and up-to-date information.

(3) That we urge the Home Missions Division and/or other interested agencies to petition the U.S. Public Health Service, to make a thoroughgoing study of peyote in all its phases;

(4) That church officials and missionary workers in the areas affected by peyote be urged to consider those ways in which education and pastoral guidance can be used in aiding our Indian people to understand and cope with this evil. Under this heading would come the "friendly approach," "the preaching of a positive Christianity," "showing a more excellent way," or similar endeavors urged by members of recent Fellowship Conferences during the discussion of peyote.

i. *Recreation Activities*

Undoubtedly the peyote cult and the use of liquor as well as the Indian ceremonial dances cater to those seeking outlets for their leisure time or to kill the doldrums of static existence. In any case Christian agencies are challenged with an educational opportunity to demonstrate that proper recreation answers human needs for creative activity and has a rightful place in building wholesome community life.

3. Federal Wardship and Full Citizenship

Wardship is the term usually used to designate the sum of legal restrictions and privileges peculiar to Indian citizens. Wardship is also a state of mind. A sense of inadequacy and fear created by prolonged and specialized protection has retarded Indian assimilation into American life. This may be overcome only as Indians are given opportunity to develop those strengths and skills and attitudes which will give them the necessary self-reliance. Any activity which gives them a chance to think and plan for themselves and to carry projects all the way through for themselves will help Indians as it helps all people to assume greater responsibilities. The challenge to us is to stimulate Indians to seize opportunities for growth. Indians must face their own failures to use all avenues open to them for self-development, and must come to the realization that the ultimate solutions to the dilemma facing them rests chiefly in their own hands. The Church must show its faith in them by giving them a responsible share in its life and work, as well as an understanding of its spirit and teaching. We rejoice in the increasing growth of Indian participation.

Federal control over Indian life must be removed as speedily as possible, first in those areas least threatening to Indian security.

Obviously no single sweeping enactment will wipe away in a moment the tangled tissue of exemptions and restrictions that has grown up through a century and a half of governmental paternalism. Old treaties have to be consummated by commutation and otherwise; land problems must be worked out tribe by tribe, often individual by individual. However, a definite goal should be set for the ultimate release of Indians from federal wardship.

Believing in Christian citizenship a definite goal should be set for the ultimate release of Indians from federal wardship. In order to achieve the end in view with a minimum of confusion and difficulty, *it is recommended* that enabling legislation cover a period of from fifteen to twenty years.

Inasmuch as suffrage has been extended to include practically all Indians, the next step would be the extension of state jurisdiction with respect to law and order. A simply worded statute somewhat as follows might be proposed for enactment into law by the Congress:

All U. S. citizens of Indian blood residing within the limits of an organized community, township, district, county, or other government unit of any state or territory of the U.S., shall be subject to all the laws—civil and criminal—of such jurisdictions in the same measure as non-Indian citizens.

4. Marriage

The widespread recognition and use of common law marriage practices makes obvious the need for social control in the interests of wholesome family life and childhood nurture. Legislation requiring the registration of all marriages within such states where none exist (for example, Oklahoma) should be given weight.

5. Civil Rights

While race prejudice between Indians and non-Indians varies according to geographical areas, backgrounds and cultural contacts, there are instances of discrimination in employment opportunities, denial of services in certain restaurants, hotels and other places of public accommodation. In view of these practices modernized civil rights statutes on the state level, including provisions for Civil Rights Commissions, adequate appropriations, power to investigate, hold hearings, negotiate with proprietors, to issue cease and desist orders enforceable in courts of law, with civil damages and denial of license to operate in cases of non-compliance, and to carry out a program of education of the public in regard to democratic, non-discriminatory services should be enacted.

6. Health

The Hoover Committee Report that "responsibility for public health be transferred to state and local governments wherever possible . . . which will help to break down the barriers between Indian and white communities" may well serve as a directive; furthermore, medical services should be paid whenever the Indian is financially able to do so.

7. Education

The emphasis should be on increasing the attendance of Indian children in public schools wherever available rather than setting up or continuing segregated schools, whether under Church or Government auspices. Pre-school and institutionalized handicapped groups represent specialized projects to which the agencies of the church must give encouragement and support.

The major objectives of mission schools should be: (1) Meeting special educational needs on a pioneer basis (for example, in the Navajo country where few public schools are available). (2) Serving to bridge the gap between boarding and public day schools on a Christian home basis. (3) Leadership training in specific fields.

8. Cultural and Religious Backgrounds

Those who work among Indians should be urged to study his cultural and religious background, to conserve such psychological and other factors which will influence their thinking and acting in becoming Christians.

PART TWO

Present Status and Extent of Protestant Missionary Work

"By our Lord's command we are to preach His Gospel to every creature. But there are some to whom perhaps we owe a peculiar and an urgent duty in this regard. Such is the American Indian." With these fitting words the Findings Committee on American Indians of the N. A. Home Missions Congress, held at Washington twenty years ago, opens its report. "Our task is preeminently spiritual," continues the findings, "the bringing of every Indian into allegiance with our Lord and Savior, for worship and service in His Kingdom, that with Christians of other races they may interpret and accept the full meaning of His Lordship in their lives."

But what of the present? Part Two of this report seeks to summarize available data which may throw light not only on present activities but suggest trends as well. Under the closing section on Program of Advance some concrete recommendations regarding the future of the work, as interpreted by the field workers, will be noted.[1]

I. CHRISTIAN AGENCIES AT WORK

1. Number

At the present time thirty-six different denominations are engaged in some form of missionary work among the Indians in the United States. Of these, fifteen are constituent members of the Home Missions Council.[2] This enumeration does not include separate societies within a given denomination as for example, American Baptist, Methodist, Presbyterian, etc., where special units responsible for mission schools, hospitals, women's work, have been set up. In addition there are a goodly number of independent or non-denominational organizations, also one inter-denominational agency, already referred to.[3]

In 1930 there were twenty-three denominations listed and six non-denominational organizations. Thus there have been thirteen denominations added to the list within the past twenty years. Included

---

[1] These were presented to the Indian Section of the National Congress on Home Missions, held at Columbus, Ohio, January, 1950, the most pertinent being incorporated in the Findings, and published in the booklet, "*For A Christian World*", 75c a copy, Home Missions Division, National Council of the Churches of Christ, U.S.A., 297 Fourth Avenue, New York 10, N. Y., pp. 49-51 and 116-118.

[2] As formerly constituted; now known as the Division of Home Missions, National Council of the Churches of Christ in the U.S.A.

[3] Under Part Six there is a listing of these by name, the reservation or tribal groups where they are at work. See Exhibit A.

31

among these are such sects as: The Four Square Gospel, Northern Gospel Association, the various Pentecostal groups, the Christian and Missionary Alliance.

Of the major denominations it is significant that there are at least three different kinds of Baptists, five Lutherans, three Methodist, five Presbyterians and three Reformed. Of the independent or non-denominational missions, the National Indian Association, an old pioneer agency, which had its origin in 1879 and was incorporated in 1887, has as its purpose: "To aid in civilization, teach industry, and give religious instruction to the Indians of our country." Known as "the oldest incorporated missionary society in America,"—1787, the Society for Propagating the Gospel among the Indians and Others in North America has had a continuous history since its organization but does not conduct any independent missions; in recent years it has become a cooperating organization with the Home Missions Council of North America.

The great majority of the independent agencies have come into existence during the past twenty-five years, notably in the Southwest. The most flourishing of these is the Navajo Gospel Mission with headquarters about fifteen miles north of Oraibi, Arizona.[4]

2. Reservations and Tribal Groups

These various denominations and societies carry on some form of missionary activity in three hundred seventy-five communities, including reservations and tribes.

This covers certain duplications inasmuch as several denominations work within one tribal grouping. Examples of this are numerous—Apache, Cherokee, Choctaw, Chickasaw, Comanche, Chippewa, Sioux, Navajo—to mention only a few. The independent agencies seem to be concentrated in the Navajo and Hopi country although by no means limited to that area.

The six regions report some form of religious ministry being carried on in 375 communities with 833 workers, including part-time, resident as well as non-resident, at 437 stations. Since the records of some agencies do not distinguish between native and non-native workers, it is not possible to list the totals under each category, only to indicate that the number of native leaders shows a marked increase during the past twenty years. The region showing the largest percentage of native workers is Oklahoma. Included in the various listings are pastors, ordained, as well as licensed, interpreters, catechists, helpers, lay readers, and local preachers. Several fields report pastors serving in the capacity of district as well as local superintendents.

The church membership as represented by the 437 stations, total 39,200 with a Protestant constituency approximating 140,000 and a total budget of not less than $1,162,939.29.[5]

---

[4] A booklet listing both by states and by sponsoring agencies—the Indian work being carried on in the various regions of the National Fellowship of Indian Workers has been prepared at the request of the National Congress on Home Missions, held at Columbus in 1950, and is available at nominal cost—Division of Home Missions, National Council of Churches, 297 Fourth Avenue, New York 10, N.Y. See Part Six, Exhibit A.

[5] A map, prepared during the summer of 1947 and revised in 1948, gives a graphic view of the number and distribution of Protestant Missions to Indians in the U. S., available at $1.50 per copy; 297 Fourth Avenue, New York, N. Y. See also Part Six, Exhibit A for a listing of location and tribal groups.

3. Number of Missions and Projects

As already indicated on page 12 this survey report covers only the fifty-nine questionnaires returned, and does not pretend to be complete. (Part Six Exhibit B endeavors to give *overall information* under six separate headings insofar as the data is available.)

For the sake of conserving space as well as convenience in referring to geographical areas the regional arrangement, already noted in Part One, is followed with statistical data included under appropriate headings.

Missions or Projects by Regions

Name of Region	Number of Denominations or Agency Reporting	Number of Missions or Projects
1. Southwest	18	73
2. Western	6	7
3. Plains	12	65
4. Oklahoma	12	53
5. Pacific Northwest	9	14
6. Eastern	2	3
Total	59	215

The number of missionaries involved in these 215 projects total 333 of which 213 are classed as native workers. Organized churches with buildings number 169 with 172 out-stations.

II. DEVELOPMENT OF NATIVE LEADERSHIP

1. To the Question—
What is being done to foster and develop a native leadership?

The Southwest Region reports:—"Through S. S. and week-day religious instruction; churches and P.-T.A., D.V.B.S."; also "an elder-ship training institute" is reported among the Pimas and Papagoes, which is rather unique and promoted by the native churches themselves. From the Plains: "Encourage higher education and special training; community work on projects;" "one sent annually to Cook Christian Training School, Phoenix." Oklahoma adds, "We send groups to state and regional conferences; also young people's camps; regular classes in Bible study."

From Wisconsin and the Bacone Conference held in 1949 respectively, come the following pertinent comments:

"Native lay leadership situation is at present very weak. One is retired because of age, one college and seminary trained licensee is in tuberculosis sanitorium. Another college man has moved to Chicago. He is teaching Sunday School in a white church. A fourth has moved out of the Indian community and is living on a farm in a white community. He comes back occasionally to assist at some special meetings but is most of the time unavailable. A fifth who was in Christian service for ten years has also moved to the city and is engaged in industry. The dispersed situation of the Winnebago makes development of native leadership very difficult. Our best young people move to the cities where they can be of no immediate service among their people."

"Different fields are developing native leaders in different ways. In the Episcopal work in South Dakota, Indians are given small part-time responsibilities in church work while they study to prepare them-

33

selves for greater responsibility. Other areas do their training in their boarding schools, working mainly with the high school students. One area reports a one day a month training school. Bacone College is offering its facilities for training programs. The Bible and other books in the native language are a great help in developing native leaders."

2. Leadership Training Facilities

In the Southwest: Tucson Training School, Rehoboth, Ganado, Navajo Bible Academy, Ignacio (Colorado) Boarding School, Farmington (New Mexico) Methodist Mission School, Cook Christian Training School, Phoenix. In Plains Region: St. Marys and St. Elizabeths Mission Schools and Hare School in South Dakota; Ashley House Correspondence Courses; "one gives four to six scholarships;" In Oklahoma: Austin Seminary (Texas), Oklahoma Presbyterian College, Durant, Bacone College, Goodland at Hugo, Friends University, Wichita, Kansas, Haskell Institute, Green Lake, Wisconsin, Oklahoma Regional Conference and Layworkers Institute. In the Pacific Northwest two say "teachers' institutes," five say, "none."

3. Courses and Institutes

Southwest: "Summer School at Santa Fe (Presbyterian, U. S. A.); short courses at Cook School; also at Flagstaff, Arizona and Flandreau, South Dakota; one reports "inter-service Bible courses every three weeks;" "Methodists have summer training institutes."

4. Plans for In-Service Training

Missionary personnel (other than above.) There is a paucity of replies under this heading. Most know of "none" at present. The Bacone Conference seminar sensed the need, couched in a very few words: "There should be more in-service training of personnel."

5. Furlough Arrangements for Workers

Majority report "none", but did mention "vacations." The Bacone seminar announced that one denomination has set its hand to the furlough plow:

> "American Baptists have furlough education for Indian missionaries three weeks at a time; also one full year after serving in 8 year periods. They also have this arrangement for all their rural workers. Some are planning 3-4 year courses for promising leaders."
> "The Methodists have the same arrangement for furloughs or Sabbatical leaves, as they do with all commissioned workers."

6. Special Personnel Problems

The opinion of those reporting under this heading are in accord with the following statement:

> "Generally speaking the churches are short of candidates for the ministry. One of the reasons for this is the lack of sermons on the ministry. There is a need for a more vigorous appeal for missionaries. Salary scales should be raised and other efforts made to make missionary work more attractive."

a. *Availability of candidates.* In the Southwest: "Candidates for Cook School too few; difficulty of getting ordained workers;" in Western Region: "have lost control of 20-30 age group;" Plains area: "small salaries encourage none but the local lay workers, often untrained," "shortage of priests and rectors;" from Oklahoma this encouraging word:

"increasing number of young people planning for Christian service, both lay and professionally."

b. *Length of service.* Southwest reports "too much turnover but a number of veterans, Indian as well as white who have sustained long-time relationship;" Plains region chimes in with "most have seen many years of service;" Oklahoma: "too short," "three couples have record of long service."

c. *Preparation*: Southwest: "slowly coming along;" Plains: Of those reporting three fields require both college and seminary training."

d. *Trends in Training Personnel*: In South Dakota, where in times past considerable stress has been placed on native churches using the Dakota (or Sioux) language the following is significant:

> "The marked change has been from the training of exclusively Dakota-speaking and older natives to read and speak in their own language to the training of younger native men through college and seminary. With these younger men the emphasis has continued to be on the use of the Dakota language with the further insistence on facility in English. In another generation in the Dakota country English can be, almost, exclusively used. In the Church schools the effort has been made to utilize native men and women in whatever minor positions possible. In one instance in the last ten years an Indian woman received appointment under the United Thank Offering program and acted as matron in charge of the Crow Creek Dormitory. In the Niobrara Deanery greater efforts are being made to secure the women and in planning the programs for an ever-increasing number of trained women workers."

III. THE CHURCH

Under this general heading are included such factors as 1. Equipment, 2. Membership, 3. Parish, 4. Sunday School, 5. Other organizations, and 6. Church Program. By its very nature the data under these respective sections must be largely statistical. However, it should be borne in mind that the adequacy of buildings and equipment as well as their proper location and use can be important factors in promoting missions; their inadequacy may prove to be a limiting factor in the Christian witness. And while membership statistics may seem relatively unimportant as such they do register a measurable allegiance to the Christian missionary enterprise. On the other hand "putting too much time on material things" can easily become a pitfall as one missionary rightly points out:

> "A questionnaire of the type you sent makes one very humble and one could feel that little was accomplished and that lives and lots of money are being wasted. We can see some progress of the Gospel but it is not by far what we would like. All too much of our time goes into material things and not enough into the direct work with the Indian in spite of the visiting we manage to do. The promotion end of the work takes too much time."

1. Equipment[6]

a. Buildings, including sanctuaries—number 162 with 96 parsonages, 52 parish halls, and 107 "other", for example Sunday Schools.

b. Types of buildings indicate that frame construction predominates (134) with brick, stone and abode next in the order indicated.

---

[6] The regional arrangement is followed in presenting the data, the same basis of representation for each area being followed as indicated on page 33.

c. The amount of land with each church or mission station varies; however, this counts up to the respectable total of 4,608 acres, of which 542 are farmed by the missionaries themselves; included in this acreage is that connected with mission schools. Practically all of this land is held by fee patent, being acquired either by grant (from tribe) or purchase. Only 17 indicate "by tenure." The latter implies — that title may be held only as long as some form of missionary and church work is carried on.

2. Membership and Attendance

These 215 projects report a membership of 15,100 or an average of 77 per congregation; services are generally conducted on Sundays, although a majority also indicate mid-week or prayer meetings as well.

It is significant that in all regions except one services are conducted predominantly in the English language which shows a marked contrast to the situation of the two preceding decades. In the Southwest however, services are predominantly in the native tongue; often interpreters are used.

Special services including evangelistic meetings as well as annual camp meetings, still play an important part in Indian missionary work. Often visiting evangelists are used, both white and Indian.[7] Confirmation classes are conducted by Episcopal and Lutheran church bodies.

3. Parish

Parish boundaries vary—from the sagebrush country of the Southwest to the cut-over timberlands of the lake states, not to mention the prairies in between. The following from Wisconsin points this out:

> "The immediate community around the church has as many as 400 or more population which sometimes dwindles to less than fifty. Three-fourths of this shifting population has no connection with the Christian Church. There are no other Protestant churches within six miles."

In Oklahoma the Indian population is "either surrounded by the whites or checkerboarded." In the Southwest the opposite is true. In the Pacific Northwest, due to migratory factors, the Indian population may be "200 in winter and 1,000 in summer."

Over-churched areas are not the rule in the Indian country, though some exceptions are cited; as, for instance, in eastern Oklahoma.

Here are some sample comments on the matter of "over-churched" or "under-churched" areas:

> Southwest: "More native churches should be established; that, in turn, depends on the success and development of the mission work; more extension work desirable in some areas; competitive efforts threaten to confuse natives."

Contributions and Benevolences.

The majority report "partial local support"; some say "enough to keep repairs up." Benevolences apparently receive more enthusiastic backing, the majority announcing "some." Indian churches do not as a rule have a budget system, with weekly envelopes, depending for the most part on "free will offerings and pledges", with tithing promoted by a minority.

---

[7] In keeping with the recommendations of the Columbus Congress a clearing house on available native workers has been prepared and may be secured by addressing Executive Secretary, Division of Home Missions, National Council of Churches, 297 Fourth Avenue, New York 10, N. Y.

It is not surprising that *home mission aid* occupies a prominent place in the financial affairs of the parish. In many cases this has been received "since organization"; in other instances "from twenty to forty years." In the Plains Region three say "sixty to seventy-three years."

Prospects for self-support vary.

In the Southwest 13 say "not yet." Oklahoma says "partial" and "not until Indians have better prospects"; Pacific Northwest "fair or moving in that direction."

Here are the additional comments under "prospects of self-support: From Oklahoma:—"Would give more if economically able"; another puts it briefly "none,—Indian will eventually be absorbed in white congregations." The latter comes from a sparsely settled Indian area where whites constitute the dominant group.

b. *Lord's Acre or other Cooperative Enterprise*

Southwest: One mission reports 70 — Lord's Acres, while still others sponsor CARE packages — for war victims sent on cooperative basis.

Plains: Seven say "no"; 3 "yes." "Approximately 5 acres set aside as church project;" "sale of quilts, clothing and gifts of produce stock;" "modified good-will industries at two points."

Oklahoma: Two say "yes, but haven't turned out so well;" however, a more optimistic endeavor, — "During last 10 years several cooperative efforts in helping to raise funds for a new church building, — all successful; church dedicated last June."

4. Sunday School

Twenty-five years ago another study of Indian religious life recorded the following:

> "The evidence of the survey shows that native Indian churches have as a rule been weak in promoting vigorous Sunday School work. This weakness has doubtless been due, in part at least, to the absence of the children at boarding schools, on and off the reservations. There has, consequently, been little incentive to conduct Sunday School for a scattered few, and when the children return in the summer little or no provision is made for their needs during the short period in which they are generally permitted to remain at home."[8]

With an increasing number of children attending public schools and others enrolled in Government day schools the situation should have been somewhat changed. There are, of course, other factors, such as week-day religious instruction, mobility of the population, bus and other transportation to non-Indian Sunday schools, not to speak of the influence of secularism common to all present-day communities.

To the question: *Is there a Sunday School enterprise?* all indicate some such activity. Of those reporting, the Southwestern region has the largest enrollment as well as the largest average attendance. This may be due to the fact that Mission Schools are furnishing the majority of teachers and leaders. Organized departments are lagging in most Indian churches although the "cradle roll" and "primary" are almost everywhere in evidence. Teacher training has come to the fore, especially in the Oklahoma area, in recent years.

---

[8] American Indian Section of Interchurch World Movement Survey "The Red Man in the United States" by G. E. E. Lindquist, pp. 395-396.

The old-type one room church school still prevails as is largely the case in other rural areas. Similarly, while there are few who observe "summer vacations", there are a number of schools not held during the coldest winter months, — especially in the Northern states.

Is there need for special courses in Indian Sunday Schools? In the Southwest "yes" provided suitable teachers are provided. At present "uniform international" lessons are largely used due, in part, to the belief that "more teachers are capable of teaching these." Graded denominational courses seem to be next in order of popularity.

Aspects of religious education which have received emphasis during the past two decades are the *D.V.B.S.* activities and the *week-day* schools. An increasing number of churches report the former as being conducted both on a union as well as interracial basis. Some regions promote special training courses for these summer Bible schools. Regional Fellowship Conference programs are taking cognizance of these training institutes as well.

Week-day classes are held both in churches and schools, depending on location. Due to recent Supreme Court decisions difficulties are experienced in use of day school buildings for week-day religious classes.

5. Other Organizations

Within the church or sponsored by the Mission are the various organizations common to all Protestants. As illustrative of this, regional reports are presented herewith:

Southwest: "Not only women's but men's sewing circles (latter among Hopis), family fun club, — all ages:" Dulce, New Mexico reports, "Home aid club for women, youth fellowship, and Girl Scouts;" Polacca, Arizona: "Nursery school, Junior Choir, 2 sewing classes;" Ganado has 4 youth groups; one Indian Fellowship and one missionary society for both men and women; 9 prayer groups." The above are typical of other regions with inevitable variations.

A mere listing of the organizations from the Plains regional area is impressive:

1. Scouts — Boys and Girls
2. Woman's Auxiliary
3. Girls Friendly Society
4. Guild,—Junior and Senior
5. Boys Crusaders
6. Mens Brotherhood; also Y.M.C.A.
7. Bishop's Committee
8. Ladies Aid
9. Brotherhood of Christian Unity
10. St. Andrew's Brotherhood
11. Little Helpers
12. Youth Fellowship — Westminster
13. Pilgrim Fellowship
14. Home Makers Club
15. Mission Health Committee

6. Church Program

Included under six headings are some items of "special work" undertaken by the church and its auxiliary societies. In order to follow the regional tabulations with some degree of clarity the questions as listed under each phase of activity are given herewith for ready reference:

a. *Missionary.*

Does this church (or churches) contribute toward the support of a native worker whether on this reservation? or for other tribes?

In the Pacific Northwest extension work carried on from the Nez Perces to neighboring tribes, especially among the Ft. Hall Indians in Idaho got under way as early as 1897. To some degree it has continued ever since. In other areas and in more recent years contributions to work among the Navajos have been made. To a limited extent tribes in the Latin American countries have also been included.

b. *Charitable and Benevolent.*

What is being done to relieve and prevent poverty?

Frequently listed as concrete efforts towards amelioration are: "Distribute clothing to needy families; cooperation with Government (Indian Service) and State agencies; furnish employment through modified good-will industries." Some indicate that their efforts are "sporadic and limited through Board of Deacons," while a lesser number "promote overall program directed toward self-support." May their numbers increase!

c. *Industrial.*

(a) What is done to *encourage thrift and saving?*
(b) Is the church sponsoring anything like a church farm?
(c) Or other enterprise aimed at helping people economically?

While some report their people as "well aware of the need to save" and as a rule "conservative spenders", others indicate that the encouragement of "thrift and saving" is very much in order and would help to foster self-support within the local church as well as in family life.

White Earth, Minnesota reports a plan which might find its counterpart in some other fields:

"Some of the farm land is being used on shares with Indian families to enable them to provide themselves with vegetables for winter use. It is hoped that most of their food for the coming year will be provided in this manner. The first attempt at this with two families was a total failure because they would not care for or harvest the garden after going to the initial work of planting it, resulting in considerable loss of seed and work to the mission.

"An attempt has also been made to furnish 8 different families with a pig each, but in all but one instance the animal was disposed of for a fraction of its value without being used by the family involved. During the past year the mission has paid Indian people almost $6000 in wages from marketing timber products such as logs, lumber, pulp, etc. It has also disposed of a considerable quantity of wild raspberries, wild rice, rugs, baskets, bird houses, and other Indian-made products for them, and has placed numbers of them in jobs such as potato picking, beet harvesting, farm hands, etc., acting as a contact between employers and Indians without charge to either party."

d. *Civic.*

What is the program of this church for interpreting citizenship to the Indians, that is, meaning of, responsibility of, developing pride as taxpayers? Inasmuch as "the rain of bullets has ceased; what about the reign of ballots?"

In view of the emphasis on release from wardship and increasing Indian participation in every aspect of American life this responsibility is being more seriously assumed than in past decades. With the return of the G. I's. the churches feel the need of stressing what American citizenship really means in exercising the right of suffrage as well as in bearing the tax load which very few escape at this time of our nation's history.

A number send "delegates to meetings where civic responsibilities are stressed"; others "present Scripture messages in keeping with citizenship." In the Southwest where the franchise has been denied until very recently, the response at general elections has been gratifying in several quarters.

e. *Off the reservation.*

What contacts have been maintained with Indians now removed from reservations?

While off-the-reservation Indians and their needs are discussed somewhat in detail under Part Three, it may be of interest here to cite what efforts the missionaries themselves feel as important to promote as part of the church program.

Through correspondence and personal visits contacts are continued to a limited degree.

From Wisconsin comes a suggestion as to "follow-up" work:

> "The pastor and parish workers visit several outside urban communities—LaCrosse, Wisconsin Rapids. A definite program of 'localizing' members who have moved away by having them join other churches and becoming active in the church life of their community in connection with any denomination if their own cannot serve them. Thus when the Lutherans in Wisconsin Rapids wanted to form an Indian Ladies Aid Society our members were urged to cooperate. Although a society sponsored by Lutherans, all officers are members of the Evangelical and Reformed Church."

In California one of the missions has launched a center in a centrally located community "to help Indians who have moved from their mountain homes to find employment and to educate their children."

f. *Special work with young people.*

This has to do with efforts directed toward reaching students returning from off-the-reservation schools, Government as well as State and Missionary institutions. Here a number of churches are eager to recognize these potential leaders by inviting them as honor guests at special dinners, fellowship meetings, picnics, games, and similar social gatherings.

There are regions, of course, where the "main issue" is to help these young people to find jobs elsewhere. Thus promising leadership in a local community is thereby "lost" through migration to some urban or industrial area.

IV. PROGRAM OF ADVANCE

1. Unreached Fields

The day of missionary pioneering in the sense of blazing new trails through forest and across prairie has largely passed. In this connection it is of interest to note that according to the 1920 Interchurch World Movement Survey there were forty reservations in eleven states, representing fifty-two tribes and tribal bands, designated as "unreached fields." This term was used to include such areas as: (1) Pagan Indians, for whom no provision has been made either by Protestant or Roman Catholic Missionary agencies; (2) tribes or portions of tribes where either Roman Catholic or Protestants, or perhaps both, are on the field but, in the words of one of our surveyors, are 'hardly scratching the surface,' reaching but a small portion of a given tribe or tribal band or where some readjustments as to allocation of responsibility are in order."

While considerable progress has been made during the past quarter century to expand the work so as to meet the needs noted above, there are today neglected and partially occupied areas which still call for church extension.

Specifically, these are largely to be found in such western states as Utah, Nevada, California, Oregon and Washington, although certain areas in Eastern Oklahoma should also be included. As recently as May, 1947, there were at least nine neglected fields in the Puget Sound region alone. These consist of small groups of from fifteen to thirty families. Among such small and scattered bands probably an itinerant ministry is needed. Following on the spot surveys (or a pooling of information already available) there should also be a pooling of personnel and funds on the part of boards and societies. It is further recommended by a number of field workers that in the interests of comity and cooperation new projects be considered on an interdenominational basis.

2. What phase of the work especially needs development within the next ten years?

To give definiteness to the needs as cited by regions there is incorporated herewith brief statements "from the grass roots observers,—the field workers themselves:

From the Southwest.

Several mention "work among men much needed:" others stress "trained native leaders and the development of youth work" with "native participation" underscored.

Western.

"Need lengthy evangelistic effort"—that is, on a sustained basis; isolated people need to be reached oftener;" in ten years Indian Office (Federal) should be closed and all attend interracial church."

Plains.

Here are varying needs succinctly expressed—

"*Church and Sunday School need strengthening.* More young people in High School developing economic independence." "Getting whites to accept Indians and Indians to reach out." *Men and buildings:* "Can't build church with preachers just serving internship;" Can't plan for future in community with buildings and equipment that give every appearance as if they were ready to pull out." "People too dependent;" "Self support;" "Cooperative aspects of Christianity should be applied to all of life."

Pacific Northwest.

Citizenship training of youth. Four list Bible study and Christian teaching as well as stewardship program. Three—release from wardship and farm aid program.

41

a. *Evangelistic Work*

Included in this section are five areas, which need development within the next ten years — the first having to do with *evangelistic work*.

While missionaries to Indians, whether pioneer or present day, have been concerned about education of the children, the healing of the sick and the comforting of the afflicted, their primary objective was and still is the proclamation of the Gospel. Stressing this basic concept the Washington Home Missions Congress of 1930 recorded the following:

> "To a greater degree than our own race, the Indian dwells in the sphere of the Spirit. His religious values should be conserved, and deepened, and related to the church life about him. Thus will he bring a real contribution to our common national life; for our missionary objective involves and must forecast his assimilation into the life of the nation, school and church."

Southwest: Stresses II Timothy 4:2

"Enlarging and making more effective program now in operation." "Camp work to be strengthened." "Visiting evangelism."

Western.

"To reach people isolated and at present unreached. To make Christian citizens."

Plains.

Present program should be kept up and strengthened." In addition, — *"The greatest need is for various denominations in the field to get together on a unified and perhaps non-denominational program of evangelism.* Whether it is possible to carry on a united work between Lutherans, Baptists and Evangelical and Reformed Churches is problematical. Evidently this cannot be effectively done on a one-way street basis. Enlistment of all Protestant churches in urban as well as rural centers to take an interest in the Indians residing in their areas and to invite them to associate themselves in an active way with church life is an ever-present opportunity and a responsibility which must not be side-tracked."

Oklahoma.

"Get children into Protestant Sunday Schools off and on Reservation."

"Reach those not served by other missions."

"Stronger religious emphasis in a non-sectarian approach to whole community."

"Deepen spiritual life of members by visitation."

Western.

"Sunday School growing so that will require new addition to church." "Training musicians."

Pacific Northwest.

"Ten per cent increase in membership through evangelistic campaign with outside speakers."

"Make church effective and self-supporting."

"Personal contact leading to Christianity."

Eastern.

Michigan, "To train young men and women in church leadership."

b. *Educational Work*

The contribution of mission schools looms large. Perhaps no other single factor has been more determinative in disseminating Christian teaching, in raising the standard of morals, and in producing a trained leadership. The mission schools have an *esprit de corps* and a personnel which bring about results even though the equipment is limited and the financial support meager. However, since 1896 when Congress ceased to make direct appropriations, the number of Protestant institutions has diminished. It should be added that this was not necessarily due to financial retrenchment but rather to a change of policy. An appreciable number of boards felt that Indian children would be better off in public schools where they were not segregated.

However, there are other specific aspects of Christian education which call for attention at the present time such as *educational evangelism, visual aids* as well as those noted in the field reports.

The field reports center around these pertinent questions: *Is there urgent need for more mission schools? If so, state reasons why. Any program for definite educational advance for the next ten years?*

Southwest.

Ten say "yes." Five say "no." Reasons—Number unschooled especially large in Navajo areas; Public schools irregular. Language difficulties acute."

Western.

Four say "no mission schools needed." "Through religious education every youth may be reached while in school."

Plains.

Three say "yes." "For finer leadership training." "To give adequate religious and secular education." "For integrating people into Amerian society." "To get grade school children admitted to public schools." "Just need week-day time release for religious education."

Oklahoma.

Seven say "no." One says "yes"

Educational Advance.

"Better attendance at district schools and to get young people into high school. Secure better qualified teachers in public schools of entire area. Some children from broken homes should be put in boarding schools."

Pacific Northwest.

Seven say, "No need for mission schools." Educational Advance: Three say most important to get them in public schools." Purpose—"To know our church, its origin, function, and faith."

c. *Social Work*

It has been said that in the old days the Indian centered everything upon his religion, which entered into every phase of his life. His planting, harvesting, feasting, recreation — in short, all interests, including health, were intimately bound up with religion. Moreover, it was felt that the young people on going home from the schools, especially of the non-reservation type, would readily fit in if there were organizations open to them for aggressive work; further that a well organized community progam on a comprehensive basis would go far towards satisfying the religious, intellectual, and social desires and longings of both old and young. Judging from field reports these basic considerations have not changed.

Among the specific items noted are a *"social program" for returned students, matron's work among Indian women and children. Religious education for youth.* Need improved church instruction in Government schools. *Train Indian mothers in childcare and unite and improve life within the home. Carry on present program of aid and visitation by missionaries. Need additional personnel for further developments.*

Western.

"As much as possible to be correlated with community projects already being sponsored locally or in adjacent areas."

Plains.

"Teach democracy and American way of life. Program for children in health training. Establish cooperative credit union."

Oklahoma.

"Friendly visits to bring Indians into contact with whole community. To build up better interracial Christian fellowship in all the areas of life, in church, business, school, home and civic affairs."

d. *Medical and Other*

The church has pioneered in medical missionary work and the contribution has been a notable one. At present there are only three hospitals in operation,—all in the Navajo country,—the Sage Memorial Hospital at Ganado, Arizona,[9] being the outstanding one. There is also one at Rehoboth, New Mexico, and at Farmington, New Mexico. Besides this, clinics and infirmaries are maintained in connection with a number of mission stations as well as mission schools and full time nurses are on the staffs.

Inasmuch as the federal government maintains seventy-seven hospitals and sanitoria and certain states have medical services available for Indians it is believed that no further expansion of hospitals as such is called for. However, present-day missions must be vigilant to promote and foster health education in homes, schools and churches, among children as well as adults. Specific aspects of extension work in some of the fields are noted herewith.

Southwest.

Dulce, New Mexico, "Indian Hospital should be reopened, now used as clinic."

"Get behind Government program (health) instead of operating hospital under mission auspices."

Plains.

"Extremely unfair to force any group of people to use one doctor, (government) who may be indifferent to their needs."

"Inform people about disease prevention and health."

---

[9] The Training School for Indian Nurses here has made a notable contribution, ably administered according to recognized standards. However, plans are now under way to stress Nurses' Aid Training.

"Include self-respect and self-decency with theme such as 'Body is temple of God'."

Oklahoma.

"Use of health slides, lectures; Government health nurse uses them once a month."

V. CHIEF PROBLEMS OF CERTAIN FIELDS AS WELL AS SUGGESTIONS FOR FUTURE

Two or three statements from as many regions tend to point up the "chief problems" on their respective fields:

1. From the Southwest

"Scattered condition of people makes work difficult and expensive."

"Isolation makes it hard to conduct services and groups of believers holding fellowship with one another."

"Reluctance of believers to put forth effort for the success of groups organized by mission workers. Successful meetings are being held in some areas, but the percentage of our membership attending meetings is still too small."

"Lack of reservation opportunity for maintaining families results in broken families as work is sought elsewhere."

"White influence and example is often detrimental."

"Drink, peyote, cited as special problems."

"Lack of enforcement of reservation law and order regulations."

"Maintenance of balance in effort directed toward children in the schools and the parents in the homes. Too often children are brought into the church school, only to have them submerged into pagan life of the homes to which they must return."

2. From the Plains Area

"Instead of the common problems of the composite citizenry of our nation we will continue to have most unfortunate special problems for our Indians until the Federal and State governments and even leading city governments unite with Christian leaders to establish an intelligent and honorable program for bringing our Indian people into self respecting, self supporting, full fledged citizenship.

"Past mistakes or broken treaties do not warrant continuing failure to lead the original Americans into the glorious liberty of true American citizenship. The newcomers from other countries learn American democracy with all its privileges and responsibilities. Why not demonstrate our leadership for the native children of our land and let the world see that we know how to be a 'good father' Nation?"

Problem number 1 is to translate *Wardship into Citizenship.*

"*Problem No. 2* is to teach these dwellers on the land to *use the land,* to raise home animals as cows, pigs, chickens and live on them; to raise garden crops and store the surplus produce for winter; to raise as much crops and stock as possible for future livelihood and insurance of protection in old age. In other words *to teach home care and industry for full personal family support.* To train the reservation folk for gardeners, farmers or stockmen.

"*Problem No. 3 to prepare those who are willing for off-reservation*

45

life. Many Dakotans are not inclined to any work that reservation life offers. Reservation land cannot yield a livelihood for their population, therefore the task of placement in city life, and labor and assistance in adjusting to the life there is an important task of Americans.

"Recognition of these social and economic problems and realization that they have a vital relationship to the ministry of the Christian Church are the fundamental responsibilities of Christian Americans today.

"Problem No. 4 naturally follows the fact that *the most energetic and alert young folks will be those who leave the home reservation and mission station.* The home church will have a struggle to *increase its giving and its progress towards self-support.* Yet this should be taught as the true Christian goal as soon as it can be attained.

"Therefore the future of any individual Indian Church is uncertain."

3. How can Mission Boards Help?

Southwest.
Nine list "more workers, trained leadership, supplies and larger budgets, greater publicity."

Western.
"More workers until adjustments are made; more time for home visits;" "higher wage levels for missionaries."

Plains.
"By helping train native leaders to operate a Government house which this community may have for the asking if same can be used for hospital or rest home." (Morton, Minnesota). "By visiting field and actually learning about problems; to make and execute plans compatible with facilities available; to interpret integration programs to congregation." "Pretty much a local problem with which we must cope." "Large investment for limited period;" "This field needs a bus badly;" "a chapter house costing $5,000," says another.

Oklahoma.
"Full support for mission program; scholarships for higher education; placing organization and responsibility on local people."

Pacific Northwest.
"Would be helpful to worker if he could be given information concerning history and conditions of the field to which he is sent as well as help to an understanding of Indian situation throughout nation as a whole." "More adequate financial support; give us *trained* workers; subsidies for youth to attend conferences; relocation of missions in certain situations; visual aids." "Enable missionary to meet needs, educational, medical, dental and clothing of his own family, with car and travel allowance *to go and go and go* without financial worries."

4. The Church and Paternalism

The question: To what extent do you feel that paternalism dominates the attitude of the church toward the Indian, either in the relation of the local church (or mission) towards the Indian, or of the home board or conference toward the local church (or mission)?

Some pertinent comments given herewith help to point up attitudes and situations:

Southwest.

Of nine reporting five say "not to any noticeable extent;" "we encourage financial independence which is first step toward total independence;" "very strong in past but we are redirecting our own missionary program toward emancipation." One field, however, feels strongly on this subject as indicated: "We are doing too much for them in some ways, — giving free of charge services which they should gradually be taught to pay for, — such services as lodging, use of electricity, linen, towels, blankets, etc." "This mission operates a community hall on a modified YMCA basis."

Western.

Two say "very little;" "church uses funds to help Indians to reach highest degree of independence both economically and spiritually."

Plains.

Eight report on this item: "We are strong for a greater measure of self-support;" "our leaders are seeking to rule it (paternalism) out and to lead the people to a willingness to assume self-support."

Oklahoma.

One suggests that the term "stepson or stepdaughter would do better;" another: "Since the Indian church surprised the sending church by assuming its share of certain projects, the paternalistic attitude quickly began to wane"; still another, less optimistic this time: "There is far more of this than the church at large realizes."

Pacific Northwest.

Six say "little or none;" "We make little of racial differences and seek to get all groups to cooperate."

47

CONCLUSIONS AND RECOMMENDATIONS[10]
PART TWO

Christian Agencies At Work

While there may be cause for rejoicing that thirteen denominational and independent agencies have launched new work in the Indian field during recent decades, nevertheless, this should be tempered by the fact that some duplication and overlapping has resulted in some areas, especially in the Southwest; moreover, since board officials as well as missionaries, have inadequate knowledge of any allocation with respect to their fields of responsibility, it is recommended that the Home Missions Division of the National Council sponsor a committee on allocation of fields which should formulate a statement of principles and procedures; (a) to guide the denominations in their relationships one with the other and in the occupancy of a given field; (b) to prepare a qualifying statement as to the meaning of the term "covering the field;" We further recommend that conferences be called to review allocation of responsibility, on a national as well as regional level, and that these be held more frequently than in the past, say every five years. Allocations should be made on the basis of survey recommendations, either already made, or in the light of conditions now obtaining in the field, such as Indian families moving away, resulting in considerable mobility, especially accelerated during the war years as well as immediately following. Specifically, these reallocations should be undertaken with the objective of avoiding overlapping and duplication of effort.

Comity and Cooperation

The facts under Religious Ministry reflect great accomplishments but not without overlapping, competition and consequent unwise expenditure of man power and mission funds in many instances.

There is a growing concern on the part of leaders in home mission enterprises that such practices have no place in the furthering of God's Kingdom. This has resulted in some outstanding examples of cooperation and mutual help in denominational approaches. Some areas of the Southwest as well as the Dakotas have pioneered in the field of Comity. More recently a great step forward has been taken in the state of Oklahoma where nine Home Mission Boards have named their representatives to a Comity Committee. This Committee has made great progress

---

10 As already noted these were presented to the Indian Section of the National Congress on Home Missions, held at Columbus, Ohio, January 1950, a number of recommendations being incorporated in the Findings, and published in the booklet, "For A Christian World", 75c per copy, Division of Home Missions, National Council of the Churches of Christ, U.S.A., 297 Fourth Ave., New York 10, N. Y., pp. 49-51; 116-118. Inasmuch as this only reached a limited number, the recommendations with pertinent supporting data are given herewith.

in facing the situations surrounding the Oklahoma Indian missions and in fostering a spirit of understanding and cooperation.

It is therefore recommended—

1. That the Home Mission Division sponsor a committee on allocation of fields, which should formulate a statement of principles and procedures.

To guide the denominations in their relationships one with the other and in the occupancy of a specific field.

To prepare a qualifying statement as to the meaning of the term "covering the field."

2. That conferences be called to review allocation of responsibility on a national, as well as a regional level, and that these be held more frequently than in the past, say every five years.

Leadership and Personnel

The Christian missionary enterprise will need, as never before, trained and fully equipped gospel messengers of both white and Indian ancestry. This calls for dedication to a long-time relationship. As already indicated adequate training should include full college and theological education with courses in religious education and with special emphasis on subjects which deal with life in a rural setting.

a. *For new recruits* every church missionary agency should prepare carefully worked-out plans for establishing contacts in the field of evangelism, camp work and pastoral visitation, meeting community-centered needs, including social and recreational.

b. *Specific types of work*

While the avenues of approach as well as the types of work may be different, the following listings may be helpful:

(1) Evangelistic work calling for ordained missionaries, Bible colporteurs, itinerant preachers and Bible teachers for house to house visitation and camp work; superintendents in charge of mission stations where there are native pastors, catechists, interpreters and helpers.

(2) Teachers of mission schools in academic, industrial and vocational subjects; adult education through night school and extension work; directors of community centers and community houses involving a social and recreational program; field workers giving attention to home economics, housing and sanitation; social case workers; deaconess work.

(3) Industrial work—farm superintendents, trained agriculturalists and mechanics.

(4) Medical work—physicians and surgeons, nurses for hospitals and field work.

(5) Religious work directors in government and mission schools and on the reservations and in Indian communities.

(6) Directors of social and religious centers in urban areas where Indians have moved in recent years; coordinators of off-the-reservation Indian work in such states as Oklahoma, South Dakota, California, Washington, Minnesota, and Wisconsin.

c. *Special leadership training*

The goal in special leadership training should be that of encouraging attendance at a recognized college or graduate school for professional and technical training. However, in certain areas and for a limited period, interdenominational training schools for Christian leadership should be adapted to meet the needs of those who for one reason or another cannot avail themselves of the above. There is also continued need in certain areas for leadership training by correspondence courses. This method has met with marked success in the Sioux country.

To facilitate more adequate and effective leadership, it is recommended:

(1) That those who work among Indians be urged to study his cultural and religious background. To that end:

(a) That a bibliography of literature on the American Indian be prepared, and reading courses based on this bibliography be required for new workers by their mission boards.

(b) That the mission boards require study at a recognized school of the cultural and religious background of the Indian group to which the new workers are appointed and linguistics for those going to areas where the native language is in extensive use.

(2) That in order to provide a manual setting forth the historical, cultural, and religious background of the Indian, especially for new workers, a revised edition of the "Hand Book for Missionary Workers Among North American Indians" be published.

(3) That Mission Boards should not only encourage attendance but provide assistance for participation in the National Fellowship of Indian Workers Conferences, regional as well as national. The programs of these conferences should be based not only on needs arising from the fields but on the larger community and world interests.

(4) That the possibilities of a field training program for pastors and lay workers on an interdenominational and interracial basis be explored.

(5) That for the next ten years at least, the Cook Christian Training School, Phoenix, Arizona, should be continued, its facilities expanded and strengthened, and its program supported by all the mission boards and societies dedicated to leadership training. We further urge that the Cook School extension courses be encouraged.

(6) That in view of the increased number of native leaders being trained for Christian service, church and community agencies be urged to give qualified leaders positions of leadership with responsibilities and salary commensurate with those given white missionaries; further, that this group reaffirm its policy in regard to the use of bi-racial leadership.

(7) We recommend that we consider favorably the appointment of Indian personnel in other than Indian fields as, for example, in schools primarily for other nationalities and races.

(8) It is recommended that under the sponsorship of the Home Missions Division a competent writer be encouraged and subsidized to write a book with popular appeal to sell the general public on the inherent virtues of the Indian and the accomplishments of the mission boards of the churches.

The Church and Christian Nurture

While missions to Indians have always been concerned about the education of the children and the ministry of healing, the primary objective has been and still is the proclamation of the gospel. To do this most effectively the paramount importance of discovering, training and using a native leadership has been recognized. The recruiting ground has not only been the mission school or the state and federal schools, but more particularly the local church. Evangelism, whether by group effort as in camp meetings, conferences, and assemblies, as well as in the personal approach, should be continued and emphasized.

In addition, we call attention to the following specific aspects of Christian education:

1. Educational evangelism should be a vital part of every church program. This is the kind of education and evangelism which takes into account the normal Christian growth of an individual and also takes into account the necessity for a thorough and conscious commitment to Jesus Christ.

2. Visual Aids. There should be an adaptation of all our Christian curriculum materials by use of pertinent illustrations from actual, everyday Indian life. Every means or method which can bring illustration into our teaching field to the advantage of our work and to encourage our Indians should be used.

3. Curriculum. Because of the similarity of our Indian problems to all life as a whole, we do not find that a definitely planned Indian curriculum as such is most desirable. Our responsibility is to plan a curriculum which would be adaptable or applicable to every Indian situation for which it is planned.

4. Each Indian Church should be definitely encouraged to have a vital program of Christian education including:
(a) Departmental Sunday School.
(b) Young People's Department.
(c) Activity groups for all ages.
(d) Vacation Church Schools.
(e) Leadership Training Program.
A committee on Christian Education in all local church bodies to give particular attention to the development of such a program.

Church Program

Rural Indian church programs must be built upon the needs of the people. The church must effect, teach and nourish an inner change in the individual members through evangelism.

Church leaders must have more training in spiritual life and know how to develop a spiritual approach and attitudes in all of the activities of the Church. The local church should be consulted in choosing a leader. Its buildings, generally limited, must be utilized to the fullest extent in carrying on the comprehensive program of the Church.

It is recommended:

1. That churches in the rural areas sincerely seek to minister in the name of Christ to *all* the people of their respective communities, and that they launch well-planned programs for meeting the basic needs of the people in all areas of life. In the distinctly Indian churches there should be a long range look toward the gradual integration of the unchurched people into an inter-racial church.

2. That, where there are white and Indian churches in the same area, they be encouraged to launch programs jointly for the betterment of the community.

3. That since there are many Indian fields now without native preachers, evangelists and other missionary personnel, the Home Missions Division provide a central clearing house for the exchange and use of such workers, wherever desirable.

4. That each church be encouraged to have a vital program of Christian education including evangelism, visual aids, adaptable curriculum, departmental church school, children's work, youth work, activities groups, vacation church schools, and leadership training.

Self-Support

Much has been said of the paternalism of the government resulting in loss of initiative, independence and self-respect. Ecclesiastical paternalism is illustrated in the subsidizing of local Indian churches and pastors—especially covering extended periods. There are instances of Indian churches receiving home mission aid for over one hundred years. One denomination came to a certain tribe years ago with the proposition that if the council would allow churches to be established, the Indians would never be asked for anything. "We will preach for you, marry you, bury you, and carry on our work for you and ask no financial support." So reads the traditional covenant. Apparently there have been unwritten covenants of a similar sort in too many Indian mission fields.

Any study of financial data will reveal that Indian churches are not well supported locally. Perhaps this is to be expected of a population predominantly agricultural in areas of limited productivity. Without a self-supporting constituency, one would hardly expect a self-supporting church. In certain areas mission-aided churches will need continuing assistance for some time to come. Having said this, one must also add that stress should be placed on the assumption of obligations—ever a prelude to freedom, which translated into present-day home mission terminology means increasing self-support as well as self-government in Christian work among Indians.

It is recommended that "target dates" should be fixed and action scheduled on the part of both mission boards and mission-aided churches looking toward complete self-support. Such fixed dates are useful for the responsible boards and societies as well as indispensable for the Indian people themselves; they will help in pointing up the thinking and in stimulating action in facing the future.

Religious Education in Government and State Schools

Religious training for children in government and state schools should be continued and extended. These institutions have always offered a challenging field to Christian service. Where government day schools are in operation, the field missionary or his assistants can and often do promote religious instruction by weekly visits. The same is true in reservation boarding schools. In more recent years similar work has been projected in public schools, especially in Oklahoma, the Dakotas and elsewhere, depending on state restrictions.

With respect to non-reservation schools, such as Haskell, Flandreau, Wahpeton, Pipestone, Chilocco, Jones Academy, Sequoyah, Albuquerque,

Phoenix, Sherman Institute, Carson and Chemawa, and more recently the new Intermountain School in Utah, the opportunity for a united approach has been especially challenging. As early as 1919 the Joint Committee on Indian Work launched the project which resulted in placing religious work directors in a number of these institutions. This represents a milestone in cooperative home missionary endeavor. Since then religious education in government as well as state schools has been expanded.

Some such pattern as worked out in the first cooperative home mission effort, already referred to above, might very well be followed in certain state schools, e.g. Thomas Indian School, N. Y., as well as so-called reservation schools, e. g. Ft. Defiance, Ft. Wingate, Tuba City in the Navajo area, Sequoyah, Concho, Ft. Sill and Anadarko, Oklahoma, etc. In addition, a relatively new field of service is presented by the work, also on an interdenominational basis, in certain hospitals and sanitoria, such as Tacoma, Washington; Talihina, Okla.; and the Sioux Sanitarium, Rapid City, S. D. (See Part Five of this report.)

* * *

Thus far we have been concerned with some of the aspects of church life and organization which were lifted out and received special consideration at the Indian seminar of the National Congress on Home Missions, held at Columbus, Ohio, early in 1950. Still others, equally important, were not dealt with specifically due to limitations of time. However, a mere listing of these items as reviewed in the body of the text in Part Two, will reveal their significance in the on-going life of the churches and their ministry. This survey has sought to present elements of strength as well as weakness as revealed from a "grass roots" vantage point. While no attempt at solution is indicated in this immediate setting these are subjects which challenge present-day missionary statesmanship and call for wise and patient leadership on the part of those charged with administrative responsibility.

In closing this section perhaps it may be well to remind ourselves of the pertinent words embodied in a pioneer study in Christian missionary work among American Indians written thirty years ago but applicable to the present:

"Those who know the Indian best—missionaries, Government officials and leading representatives of the Indian race—are the least inclined to sentimentalize over him. To the vision of such friends, unobscured by romantic fancy or antiquarian zeal, the Indian appears not as an interesting relic of the past, but as a future citizen, at present in a difficult stage of transition, but destined ultimately to be merged, like other racial groups, into the population of the country. Like those other groups, the Indian has his own contributions to make to the body politic. . . . . The religious instinct is of the very fibre of the race. The crude Messianic beliefs prevalent among many tribes responded readily to the teachings of the early missionaries.

"In spite of the secularism and neo-paganism of American society as a whole, the Indian of today will continue to respond 'by outward and visible signs' to the 'inward and spiritual grace' bestowed upon him through increasing knowledge of the word of the 'Great Spirit'."[11]

---

[11] Lindquist, G. E. E. "The Red Man in the United States," op. cit. p. xiv.

PART THREE

The Church and the Indian in Urban Centers

The Church has long been conscious of the great needs confronting the Indians living in the urban centers of America, and upon many occasions has voiced appeals, through various National and Regional bodies, for more diligent and concerted efforts toward helping those individuals meet their new situations.[1]

Looking toward the Home Missions Congress in 1950 it seemed wise to make a more detailed study of the actual social, economic and spiritual conditions of these migrated Indians, in order to afford a basis for a more intelligent and practical effort to meet those needs now existing. In order to determine what the local urban situation is in reality, and to learn if the local church forces of those areas are meeting the social, economic and spiritual problems of the Indian people, a study of one particular urban center was undertaken. The city of Rapid City, South Dakota, was chosen because it was felt that in that place could be found a pattern which is more or less true of *all* urban areas where Indians are to be found.

It was felt by the Survey Staff that in order to understand and fully appreciate the true conditions of the Indian people in a city, such a study should proceed as follows:

1. A history of the city under study which would throw light upon existing white attitudes.
2. The geographic and social backgrounds of Indians involved.
3. The Indians' cultural surroundings, including their educational status, any racial feelings reflected by their white neighbors, their working conditions, degree of assimilation, group participation, etc.
4. The degree to which they have been assimilated into the existing churches and the degree to which the churches of the community have ministered to their needs.

To accomplish this end three steps have been followed:

1. Careful observation of the city under study.

   To roam the streets, sit in hotel lobbies, listen to conversations on city buses, eating places and retail stores, etc., one will learn a great deal about the situations surrounding a less privileged group of people in any city.
2. Use of questionnaires measuring racial attitudes. (See Appendices *B* and *C*)

---

[1] See also *"Indians In Urban Centers"*, A Manual for City Pastors, Religious Educational Directors, Church Social Workers and Directors of Social Agencies by G. E. E. Lindquist, published by the Home Missions Council of North America at 7 Winona St., Lawrence, Kan., 1948. 10c copy.

This method was used to some extent in the study. The above mentioned questionnaire was submitted to several large groups of people. Another questionnaire was submitted to the city pastors, and was designed to measure the extent to which the church had endeavored to meet the Indian's needs.

3. Personal visitation with the Indian people themselves.

It seems certain that as far as the Church is concerned two major things may develop from such a study:

1. Through a correlation of existing situations both in the city and back on the reservation, the entire reservation mission program may be reevaluated in terms of its efficiency and help in preparing the Indian for the new day ahead of him.

2. The findings of such a survey should clearly point the direction of the development of a program on the part of the city church as it becomes more fully aware of the needs of the Indian people within its area.[2]

I. THE URBAN COMMUNITY UNDER STUDY

Rapid City, South Dakota, was chosen for this study because the Indian situation there is typical, on a larger scale, of what is happening generally in towns and small cities on the fringe of reservation areas.

Rapid City is not unlike many other communities of America in many respects. It has its small industries, including lumber mills, a cement plant, flour mill, pottery plant, a novelties plant, wholesale houses, a wood working industry, etc.

It has its ambitious Chamber of Commerce which "points with pride" to the city's natural beauty, its entertainment features, including its taverns, night spots, beautiful parks, swimming pool, motion picture theaters, and "attractive dance emporiums." Also mentioned are "the Indians who may be seen daily on the streets of Rapid City at any time of the year. Some may be found living in their native fashion and observing native customs of dress and living." Much space is given to advertising the "Indian show which is staged — free to the public — in front of Duhamel's at 7:00 each evening."

Due to its peculiar geographical location Rapid City enjoys a prosperity many cities might envy. Due to the fact that it is considered the gateway to the Black Hills region it has become a great wholesale distributing center as well as a famous tourist attraction.

There are but very few foreign-born residents of the city, only a dozen Negroes, but as many as 3000 Indians from nearby reservations, chiefly the Pine Ridge, Rosebud and Cheyenne River.

There are twenty-four churches in Rapid City, including most of the "major" denominations, to which have been added others usually thought of as the more emotional, evangelistic sects.

Rapid City has suffered the same as any other due to its rapid growth. Its current population of 26,600 reveals a rapid growth since 1930. At that time there were 10,404 residents of the city, and in 1940 there were 13,844.

---

[2] See map on p. 119 "Cities indicating Appreciable Indian Population; also Church Organizations At Work.

The visitor soon gets the feeling he is in a western town. The sun-bronzed faces of all he meets on the streets, the cowboy boots and sombreros on the men, the wind-swept and dusty streets, the cafe conversations dealing with "cattle", and "the ranch", the slow tempo of life and the ready friendship of the Rapid City natives all attest to the fact the West has truly begun. To this picture one should add the eastern and far-western tourist, the stop lights, the bombers overhead from the nearby air base where can be seen the world's largest hangar, and the streamlined city buses, and there is created a peculiar mixture of East and West.

History of the Indian-White Contact

To understand the present situation one must understand the developments leading up to it. This city had its origin in the gold rush of the late 19th century. With the discovery of gold came the great influx of prospectors from the east as well as from Denver and Cheyenne.

But there were Indians in this territory long before that time, and the Black Hills region was their favorite hunting grounds. It was well known that the Hills were a part of the then enormous Sioux Reservation, set apart by treaties and in part, by Presidential Order. With the influx of prospectors protests were made to Washington and some promise was made to remove the miners from certain areas of the Hills. Suffice it to say, however, the miners were not removed, the Indians were subsequently confined to smaller reservation areas, and have been waging a periodic but losing legal battle in their Black Hills claims.

Any community populated by the descendants of these early mining pioneers will be greatly affected in their attitudes toward any Indian coming into their midst. This particular community is no exception.

Prior to the late war the Indian population was such as to cause no apprehension or concern. Occasionally small bands of Indians would come to town, either at the invitation of the Chamber of Commerce to dance in a ceremonial designed to attract the tourists, or individual Indian families who had as their purpose the buying of provisions. Even those families coming to town to live would soon go back to the reservation areas.

Later, with the development of small industries, the opportunity for wage earning began to attract the Indians from surrounding areas. At the same time the operators saw a great wealth of cheap labor. This resulted in an increased influx of resident Indians who were, generally speaking, relegated to the least desirable living quarters of the city.

In the early years of the present decade came World War II, and we know what happened in nearly every locality in America, a great surge of people descended upon the cities. War industries attracted large numbers of people to the urban centers, there to establish more permanent homes. The Indians were included in this migration, and numbered in the many thousands. What is happening to these Indians at the present time is a grave concern to a large number of persons who are anxious for their continued development and welfare.

II. THE INDIAN IN RAPID CITY
Population and Location

Such a study as undertaken is a difficult one due to the fact that the Indian population is such a shifting one. Dr. Carl Watson, a long time

56

resident of the city, stated it this way, "Any census taken today will be obsolete tomorrow. . . The police are sending Indians out of town everyday, but many of them return the next under another name."

Reservation ties are very strong with many, and there is much traveling back and forth with the seasons. In view of this fact an estimate of numbers is about all that can be done. One estimate places the number of Indians in Rapid City at 3,100, others as low as 2,000. Somewhere between those figures will be found the average.

These Indians are to be found in nearly all parts of the city, there being no zoning ordinances to restrict their housing quarters. In general, however, they are located along Rapid Creek and adjacent blocks either way, extending from 1500 West and eastward about twenty blocks. This area at its midpoint approaches the business section on the north. There is also a small island known as South Camp on the southeast edge of the city.

Economic Conditions

"The urge for Indians in the Dakota Country to leave their reservations to find work is very real. It is estimated that the resources of the Indians at Pine Ridge will support less than half the tribal population."[3]

In the final analysis, the major reason the Indians are now in the city is largely an economic one. The reservation system is in trouble because the land will not support the growing population. Many Indians will not adapt themselves to a farm culture, and many now want to find a bridge between their old nomadic life and the new stability of a weekly paycheck.[4]

Although the trend has been in progress for several years, it was greatly accelerated by the establishment of the war industries. Development of air fields, depots, and other industries presented a much needed opportunity for wage earning. This had a double effect. It gave the Indian some foundation for feeling wanted and needed in the community, as well as an experience in living in close association with whites. It must be said that this experience has not always been successful or happy. Those who came to the war industries received the highest incomes and enjoyed the best food, clothing, and living conditions in their entire experience.[5] At the same time there is witnessed a withdrawal from, or a postponement of, participation in the agricultural economy of the reservation.

A study of "off-the-reservation" Indians made in 1941, showed a wide variation in success in working and living among whites. Some had done well in their jobs, and, by proving their ability to do skilled work, had advanced in their occupation. More showed instability by moving from job to job or by going back to the reservation often.[6] This is true of Rapid City.

It is the weighted opinion of many that the Indians, with their native artistic abilities and skills as craftsmen, have little difficulty in secur-

[3] Lawrence Lindley, "Uprooted Indians", *Indian Progress*, May, 1949.
[4] Associated Press, May 3, 1948.
[5] Gordon MacGregor, "Warriors Without Weapons", p. 201, University of Chicago Press, Chicago, Illinois, 1946.
[6] MacGregor, "Wartime Employment of the Rosebud Sioux", p. 302.

ing and progressing in their jobs. This is in spite of the fact they are often excluded from membership in most AFL Unions. The C.I.O. is more liberal, and the industries dominated by the C.I.O. unions have been much more generous in accepting Indians.

Mr. Frank McConnell, of the Rapid City Indian Welfare Association, stated, "If an Indian is worth $1.50 per hour, that is what he gets. There is some industrial discrimination, mostly at the lumber mill, but the Indian is easily discouraged. He gets a job, goes to work, he does something wrong, the boss bawls him out. About the second time this happens, he hits the Creek (referred to the Indian Camp on Rapid Creek), he begins to drink, he beats his wife, she leaves him, or a family honestly tries to make a go of it but fails. They come to me and say 'We can't make a go of it, get us back home'."[7]

A more detailed analysis, based upon visits with 136 families, made by Rev. Levi Roulliard formerly of the Home Missions Council staff,[8] shows the following occupations:

Laborers—66	Nurses—2	Heavy Equipment
Machinists—9	Janitors—2	Operators—2
Service Station	Retired Ranchmen—3	Plasterers—1
and Garage Men—3	Pensioners—2	Beautician—1
Carpenters—4	Farm Worker—1	Seamstresses—2
Ward Attendants—2	Plumbers—3	Retired Gov. Employees—2
Stockroom—1	Housekeepers—9	Soldiers—4
Cafe Workers—6	Painters—4	Laundry Operators—6
		Gardener—1

A greater percentage of Indians work in the large lumber mills which own the land on which many of them live. Others are employed in slaughter houses, packing plants and other work of temporary nature, and with lower incomes being paid. This remark of a lumberman was overheard while sitting in a hotel lobby in Rapid City in 1946, "I have no labor problem. I can hire all the Indians I want for 45 cents an hour." It was observed that many of the women in the "Camp" receive "ADC" (Aid to Dependent Children) from the state.

It can be generally stated that the Indian's work is either so uncertain or of such a nature that some citizens of the community share the opinion of a barber as he remarked, "What do they do? Nothing! I don't see how they get by! They won't work — lay around in their old dirty clothes. Seems that's just the way they want it — most of 'em. Can't hire one to turn a tap — won't work!"

Housing

Closely connected with the economic condition of the Indian people is the matter of housing which often reflects the economic standing of a family. One can see some of the best and some of the worst in Rapid City.

The Rapid City Indians fall into three general classes:

(a) The "Camp" or "Tent" Indian.

---

[7] Statement to author.

[8] Rev. and Mrs. Percy Tibbets, both of Sioux descent, are now occupying the position formerly held by Mr. Rouillard and are promoting a community project with the aid of a representative local committee.

Scattered along Rapid Creek for almost the breadth of the city is
the Indian camp where most of the early arrivals take up residence.
Here are the tents, most of them without floors, no sanitary facilities
except privies along the creek bank. Since the camp is in the creek
valley, mud and slush is abundant. There are many children, large
numbers being out of school. The school superintendent stated it was
extremely hard to keep track of the children since there was so much
going back and forth from the reservation. Many of the men have
worked at the near-by lumber camp, and buy provisions at the company store. Wages paid at the lumber camp are acknowledged to be
lower scale than other industries in town.

It cannot be said to be a strictly Indian camp, since there are several families of white people living in the same area. Feeling between
the groups is cordial.

Rents even for tent space are high. It was stated that rent for tent
space alone is $3.00 per month. One room shacks and small cabins rent
for $10.00 to $25.00 per month. The land on which the camp is located is owned by the lumber company.

(b) The "Shack" Indians.

Some have been able to move into the small shacks scattered among
the tents. Here the conditions remain unchanged, except they are not
so exposed to the elements, a no small factor in the South Dakota
winters. It should be stated that among the shack dwellers, some
shacks are clean, with some effort being made toward beautification.
Little evidence of building repairs can be seen.

(c) The "House" Indians.

Surrounding the camp, and on the streets above the creek bottoms
are to be found the small homes of those who have come to be known
as the "House Indians." Many of them are owner-occupied by those
Indians who have been in the city for longer periods of time. Many
of these people are active in community affairs, and are looked upon
as respected citizens. Many of these homes are exceptionally clean and
neat.

A survey of Indians in Rapid City was made in 1948 by Miss Della
Ryan, Government Indian social worker at that time from the Billings
Area Office, and Mrs. Ruth K. Heineman, social worker at the Pine Ridge
Agency. Mrs. Heineman said that the survey showed that the very evident
Indian population along Rapid Creek constitutes only about one-third of
that of the city. Another third has lived there for eight to twenty years
and has become quite adjusted to city life. This third has regular employment, owns its own home or lives in comfortable rented houses; their
children are in school regularly and they are fairly well integrated into
the life of the community. The other third of the Indian population is
between these two. They have been living in Rapid City for three to
eight years. Their reservation ties are sufficiently broken so that they
return only for brief visits, family gatherings or tribal affairs. They are
not fully integrated into the life of the city, but they are moving in that
direction, and in a time of very high employment they manage to care
for themselves most of the time in a fairly satisfactory manner.

In noting the housing conditions of the 136 families mentioned
above, the following seems pertinent:

No. of families living in tents _____ 41
No. of families living in shacks or trailers _____ 35
No. of families living in houses _____ 40
No. of families living in rented rooms _____ 20
No. of families living in their own homes _____ 14

It must be noted, however, that in all the above categories there were to be found white families living as neighbors and sharing the same economic conditions as the Indians. One Indian woman in the "Camp" said, "We have some good white neighbors and we visit a great deal." In the city the average length of residence of those living in tents as compared to that of Indians living in houses, the following throws an interesting light.

Those in tents _____ 3.29 years in Rapid City
Those in houses _____ 10.94 years in Rapid City

One must thereby assume that the urban Indian can and often does better his economic condition the longer he remains in the city. Those in the less desirable situations are more often those most recently arrived in the city.

Confining our consideration to the locality under study the following general observations can be stated:

The majority of Indians enter the lowest strata of white culture, many of them to remain there. Coming to town with little money they are forced to live in the poorest rooming houses and sometimes in auto courts. Only when they have achieved better paying jobs can they move to better quarters.

There are those who fail to form attachments to either respectable white or Indian society in the towns and yet do not want to return to the reservation. These people drift to the bottom of the social order. Caught up with the worst element of the white or Indian slums, they live in the shoddiest rooming-houses or Indian camps at the edge of town and frequent the cheapest beer joints, dance halls, and other gathering places of slum dwellers. Often they are picked up for delinquency or vagrancy. They are thereafter considered delinquents, but more correctly they are the victims of their own difficulty in finding any place in either Indian or white society.[9]

Although the majority of Indians may enter the social scale on the lower strata, a large number have been able to progress to higher strata within the stratification of the white urban community. In a recent Associated Press article it was stated, "In their climb from semi-savagery to what we label civilization, they go through three stages—they are known as tent, shack and house Indians.

"The tent Indians are a sad caricature of their ancestors. They are sheltered by canvas tents instead of skin tepees. They try to live on the original Army "K" rations — balls of pounded suncured meat mixed with dried fruit and tallow and eaten with dried corn. As they progress, the tent Indian builds shacks of boxed and scrap wood. Then the more ambitious save money and build modest wooden houses like the workers do."

There are others who are able to enter the scale at a rather high point because of wealth, intermarriage or previous off-reservation experience elsewhere. Among this group primarily is to be found a higher degree of participation in white organization, cultivation of white friends, intervisitation with white neighbors, etc. In many instances there can be seen a cleavage between this group and those Indians in a less assimilated state.

---

[9] MacGregor, "Warriors Without Weapons", op. cit., p. 151.

In a number of states "Indians-off-the-reservation" are not welcome in the better hotels, the better restaurants, the better stores. Many of the towns where this segregation takes place border larger Indian reservations and are economically dependent on Indian trade. . . Indians who go to many cities to work find that they must accept housing in the slums, for they are not wanted in the better parts of the city. They are not welcome in the better churches; their children are often not encouraged to attend public schools; they are not welcome in the better hospitals; they are often excluded from the better theaters.[10]

There is a group of whites to whom the Indians, especially the mixed bloods, are more acceptable. This group is composed of poorer farmers and townspeople, often those who live on "the wrong side of the tracks." "Because of the greater freedom of social relationships with these white people, the Indians are adopting their patterns of living, their social attitudes and values. The Indians are merging to a greater degree with the lower class. At the same time the tradespeople, well-to-do farmers, and government employees, who form the middle class of such states as Nebraska and South Dakota, look upon the Indian as socially and economically inferior. The Indians who are acceptable are those whose *education, employment*, and *social behaviour* are like their own."[11]

Attitudes of the Indian

Generally speaking, the attitudes of the Indian people toward their present situation might well be classified in the following categories:

a. Many Indians express resentment of the white man's expectations of him.

Due to his relatively short period of transition from a more primitive culture, coupled with the inability of the white population to disassociate the younger Indian from the traditional conception of Indians, the Indian people often find themselves unable to conduct themselves as other citizens of the community. Many of them find themselves in the position of one Indian student who remarked, "My number one problem is that white people insist I act like *they* think an Indian should act!" The above mentioned activities of the local Chamber of Commerce is resented by a great number of the more highly cultured and adjusted Indian people.

b. There are those in the community who express resentment against certain activities of the city which reflect upon their rather deplorable economic state. News items and pictures in the local and state papers have aroused rather bitter feelings.

c. Those with the "persecution attitude."

In the minds of many of the less favored Indians of Rapid City is the first conviction that because of being Indian they must always battle unfavorable odds if they are to ever get ahead. Said one shack dweller, "The Indian is getting a bad break. He has to fight for all he gets."

d. Those expressing optimism and encouragement.

One Indian said, "The Indian's number one problem is himself. There is nothing in Rapid City which would prevent an Indian from going any-

---

10 Willard W. Beatty, "Indian Education", No. 150, published by the Education Branch, U. S. Indian Service, Department of the Interior, Washington, D. C.

11 MacGregor, op. cit., p. 206.

where and accomplishing any purpose except his own inability to adjust. . . The Indian's great need is organization with sensible leadership. . . an organization including whites and dedicated to working with the whites and not fighting them all the time. . . The Indian only needs to prove himself, and he is accepted." One need not comment that the latter Indian is a perfectly adjusted one who holds a responsible position and highly respected in the community.

Although it must be considered natural that any group of people from similar backgrounds choose to associate with each other, the majority of younger Indian people deplore racial segregation. However, there are understandable reasons why there are, as a rule, to be found such organizations as Indian Clubs, Indian churches, and in many cases organizations within the existing white organizations which in special ways appeal to the Indian people. The social isolation experienced by Indians newly arrived in cities is very discouraging. Just as young rural white people just arriving in the city tend to be together, the Indian people are very hesitant in breaking into the existing white cultural units. Quite often the Indian dweller in the city foregoes associations within the city, and continues his contacts with groups back on the reservation. This is especially true of his church affiliations.

Surveys by several individuals tend to establish the fact that in general the Indian does not participate in the white-dominated activities of the city. There are, of course, outstanding exceptions in all areas, especially in those cities adjacent to, or a part of, a highly assimilated Indian area.

Where these exceptions occur, it is significant to note that the degree of participation is closely connected with the age of the Indian and his length of residence in the city. In MacGregor's study of 1946 it was pointed out that the older Indians moved into good neighborhoods and participated in white society only after years of residence in the larger centers.

There are to be found Indians who have been able completely to bridge the existing gap between the two cultures and have become completely adjusted.

Community Attitudes

Of course one will find the same variations in community attitudes toward the Indians as towards other racial or social groups, but this fact should be established — the Rapid City citizens reflect a cordial feeling, and a high respect and spirit of good will, toward the Indians in their community. It is true, this feeling has not been often expressed in terms of positive betterment projects, but it is quite evident that they are exercising no active dislike. As a matter of fact, on the basis of the racial attitudes questionnaire submitted to several groups of people, all white, one must draw the conclusion that the Indian enjoys a rather high rating as compared to some other racial groups. In compiling the returns of the 100 questionnaires, in all but one case every check was in the upper half of the sheet, indicating friendliness and good will, one designating willingness to marry, and all stating they would include Indians as personal friends.

Generally speaking, citizens of Rapid City are saying, "It is not a racial problem exclusively. It is an economic and social one. From every Indian excluded from certain community activities, there are as many or more white people — both of them on the grounds of sub-standard economic conditions." This would tend to substantiate the opinion stated above by one Indian that the answer to the Indian's problems lies in part, at least, with the Indian himself.

Antagonistic feelings do exist, however, and must be taken into account. There does exist the feeling on the part of one or two city officials that Rapid City was being asked to shoulder responsibilities not rightfully theirs. They feel the Indian is a full responsibility of the Federal Government, that he has no right to be away from the reservation, and that he should be sent back there to be "rehabilitated."

Probably the best summary of the community attitude toward the Rapid City Indian was included in a conversation with the City Attorney: "I've been interested in Indians all my life. We have a problem on our hands in Rapid City, but progress is being made. Old timers tell us that years ago nothing was seen but blanket Indians, speaking no English. Today we see them in clothes, speaking English. Their daughters are dressed nicely, working in the stores and cafes. . . But the problem of the camp Indian now in the city belongs to Rapid City, and the city officials, the citizens, and organizations must accept this responsibility. The Church must face the problem too. We need more recreation.[12] The Indian children should be more in our public schools rather than government schools, and the parents must assume more responsibility for community welfare."

An outstanding woman of the city, long active in the Indians' interest, stated, "These Indians prove over and over that there is a wide-open opportunity for any who desire to get ahead and become acceptable members of our community. It can be done, and I have seen it happen many times."

III. THE CHURCH AND THE RAPID CITY INDIANS

Broad statements are dangerous, but it can be said that the Protestant churches of Rapid City, as is generally true in all urban situations, have almost completely failed to meet the needs of the Indians. One or two exceptions should be mentioned. The Episcopal Church reports forty-seven Indian families as members of the church with from twenty-five to thirty-five individuals rather faithful in attendance. Rev. Levi Rouillard, former Home Missions Council worker for "off reservation" work, states he has always felt accepted and appreciated. The Wesleyan Methodist people have constructed a small, neat chapel in the Camp but they limit their program largely to "saving the Indian's soul."

The Presbyterian and Congregational churches say they "believe there are some of their people in the city but they do not know how many nor where they are."

---

[12] Plans are under way whereby the Interdenominational Work Camp Committee, which represents the United Christian Youth Movement and the Youth and Student Committee of the Division of Home Missions, may sponsor a work camp in Rapid City during the summer of 1951, with special emphasis on recreation and similiar activities.

A questionnaire was submitted to the ministers of the city in an effort to determine the extent to which the church has gone to the Indian people, as well as the attitude of the white members, should Indians come into the church. The results of this questionnaire are as follows:

Number of Questionnaires returned	9
Number of churches reporting Indian members	5
Total number of members	207
Number of churches reporting pastoral calling on Indians	6
Number of churches reporting having invited Indians to attend	8
Number of churches reporting Indians participating in church activities other than congregational worship	2
Total number of Indian attendance in all churches reporting	85
Number of churches stating an attitude of friendliness	6
Number of churches stating an attitude of indifference	3
Number of pastors expressing opinions that Indians should attend distinctly Indian churches	2
Number of pastors expressing opinions that Indians should attend established churches	7

There is a very distinct line drawn between the Rapid City churches. On one side will be found the more evangelistic churches such as the Assembly of God, the Open Bible Church, Pentecostal, etc., the ministers of which form the Ministerial Association. On the other side will be found the Methodist, Congregational, Lutheran, Presbyterian, Baptist and Episcopal, whose ministers and laymen form the County Council of Churches.

A very sympathetic attitude and a real concern that some program of action be started has been expressed by the County Council of Churches. An Indian Committee has been appointed with the responsibility of organizing and carrying forth a complete Indian Religious survey in order to first determine the actual situation. It is acknowledged that most of the Protestants in Rapid City are Episcopalians. The percentage of Congregational and Presbyterian adherents is being determined.

There is some feeling among the Episcopal group, both Indian and white, that an Episcopal chapel should be constructed near the Indian camp. A strong plea was placed with Bishop Roberts[13] that should this be done, it not be designated as an *Indian* church, but that it be open for all residents of that mixed community. To this suggestion he readily and enthusiastically agreed, going even further to indicate that such facilities might well be available to other religious groups caring to use them.

This feeling has grown and there are many opinions expressed by both Indians and whites that the Indian will not attend the city church in which he feels uncomfortable and perhaps unwelcome. As quoted elsewhere, one Camp dweller stated: "We won't go to town to church.

---

[13] Rt. Rev. W. Blair Roberts, Episcopal Bishop of South Dakota.

We don't feel at home. We can't dress up and don't like to walk down the aisle. . . Ministers of most churches will not come down here and live as one of us. . ." Said an influential white citizen: "It is absurd to expect the majority of those Camp Indians to come into our city churches at this stage." However, a number of Indians who have lived for some time in the city and have succeeded in establishing themselves as active members of the Episcopal Church, registered strong protest at the establishment of another *church*, feeling that there was strong danger of its becoming a racial church. It is felt by some authorities that should a racial church develop this particular group of Indians will drop completely from church activities due to an increased pressure from the other Indian people to attend the Indian Church. It is feared that, coupled with this, will be the feeling of certain white people of the church that "these Indians should attend their own church now that they have one."

A bit of encouraging information was to the effect that the Men's Brotherhood of the Methodist church, working through the Winona Club, is planning to finance the construction of a laundry and shower house in the camp area. A small beginning, to be sure, but a most practical and vital one. This idea has more recently been incorporated in a unified and expanded program under the sponsorship of the County Council of Churches, The State Council of Churches, and the Division of Home Missions National Council of Churches.

One may well ask the question, "Is adjustment to city life possible for an Indian?" To those who insist upon pointing to the Indian who repeatedly falls into the lowest social stratum, the answer will probably be "no." But to others who have confidence in the Indian's ability, as well as those with a sense of fairness, usually manifested by the American citizens, the answer is "yes." They restate the fact that the Indian may become adjusted to urban life even as he has become adjusted to modern civilization. Indians need not and do not become misfits simply because of their racial heritage, but rather because of certain social deficiencies common to representatives of all races.

Conclusions and Recommendations

1. There has been a lack of coordination and communication between the reservation mission program and the work of the city churches and other city agencies. This often resulted in the Church finding itself in the position of spending large sums of money for a reservation mission program, often including in that program certain phases which encourage the Indian to leave the reservation, but failing to meet the Indian's problems when he arrives in the congested urban areas. Thus the Church often fails the Indian when he needs the help the most. It often appears to be a case of participating in a worthwhile cause, but stopping at the wrong point. It should be the responsibility of the reservation missionary to advise the ministers of their city churches as to the arrival of their Indian people and how they might best serve them.

2. The difficulty in personal adjustment is evidence that the reservation mission program has often been lacking in the teaching of Indian people, about to leave for the cities, what they are going to experience and

how they might best take care of themselves in their new experiences. One of the "real cures" for their present problems might well have begun before they ever left the reservation area. One often hears the statement, "These Indian people often land in town unprepared for what they are to experience. The real cure for their present problems could well begin out there on the reservation." Classes in adult orientation and personal adjustment should have a real place in any reservation mission program.

3. The city churches, by the same token, must accept a broader interpretation of their duties, opportunities, and obligations regarding the people of their community, Indian or white. Very little lasting contribution will be made by the Church toward lifting the Indian from the creek bank to a respected place in the community as long as it limits itself to a preaching program alone. Personal visitation is highly important, but it should go much farther than that. It must ultimately include such activities usually associated with the Settlement House. The "laundry house" idea is a good start but should be expanded to include classes in home betterment, job placement, child-care classes, health improvement, recreation, etc. Such a Center should never supercede the Church, but should be used as a means and a channel through which the Indian people could be contacted, befriended, trained, and ultimately directed into the existing churches and other community activities. Such a project has been tried in several areas, Los Angeles, under the Friends Church, and Phoenix, Arizona, under the auspices of the Home Missions Council. (See Appendix A for further information).

4. Such an approach should be based on two conditions:
   a. It should not be on a segregated basis, but rather as an arm of the Church extended to a group of needy people, *both Indian and white*, living in substandard conditions. It should again be noted that we cannot truthfully say this is an "Indian" problem alone. It is an economic problem involving groups of people regardless of racial lines. The Christian Church should face its responsibilities on this basis.
   b. Should the Church approach the problem on a scale necessary for success, it should be on a cooperative basis rather than on a competitive, denominational one. Where success has been achieved to the greatest degree it has been in places where local Councils of Churches, Ministerial Associations, or other cooperative agencies have approached the problems on a level of cooperation.

5. The conditions of the Indians in the cities are not totally discouraging. It is quite evident the problems can be worked out because they *have* been solved in hundreds of cases of Indians, who through education and active Christian living, have proven themselves able and acceptable. However, a staggering task remains to be done in educating both the Indians and the white people as they undertake the process of adjusting to each other. The Indians must be awakened to their true worth, and must have recreated within them a spirit of confidence and worthwhileness. On the other hand, it is highly necessary that stereotypes be destroyed in the minds of the white people, and that they, too,

be trained in the true nature and worth of the Indian as an individual. Such an educational task must be assumed by the Christian forces of any community.[14]

[14] The basic recommendations as given above were incorporated in the Findings of the Indian Section of the Columbus, Ohio, Home Missions Congress, already referred to, and listed on p. 50 of the booklet, *"For A Christian World"*, which is the report of the entire Congress and may be obtained from the Division of Home Missions, National Council of Churches, 297 Fourth Ave., New York 10, N. Y., at 75c per copy.

APPENDIX A

Indian Service Center Statistical Report for year 1948

Phoenix Arizona Attendance Record

January	577			July	598	year to date	4396
February	621	year to date	1198	August	758		5154
March	584		1782	Sept.	867		6021
April	689		2471	Oct.	731		6752
May	794		3265	Nov.	670		7422
June	553		3718	Dec.	832		8254

Showers

Two showers were installed, one each in the two rest rooms. They were put into use the latter part of May. Due to the vacation schedule reports for June and July were combined.

June-July	68			Oct.	41	year to date	162
August	22	year to date	90	Nov.	40		202
September	32		121	Dec.	50		252

Break Down of Registration Cards

Total number of individual Indians registered _____ 1989
    Tribes represented

Tribe	No.	Tribe	No.	Tribe	No.
Pima	667	Spokane	2	Mojave-Papago	4
Navajo	216	Isletta	2	Pima-Mexican	5
Maricopa	172	Yakima	2	Maricopa-Yuma	4
Hopi	108	Otoe	2	Pima-Navajo	3
Not Given	108	Piute	2	Maricopa-Navajo	3
Papago	72	Iowa	2	Hopi-Navajo	3
Apache	67	Little Lake	2	Papago-Maricopa	3
Yavapai	43	Chimehuevi	2	Pawnee-Chickasaw	3
Sioux	40	Concow	2	Pima-Mission	3
Mojave	34	Cheyenne	2	Cherokee-Hopi	3
Yuma	20	Klamath	2	Mission-Papago	2
Walapai	18	Pomo	1	Pima-Osage	2
Sac & Fox	11	Acoma	1	Cherokee-Navajo	2
Cherokee	11	Arapahoe	1	Navajo-Apache	2
Choctaw	7	Osage	1	Pawnee-Mojave	1
Nez Perce	6	Mexican	1	San Juan-Pueblo	1
Chippewa	5	Bannock	1	Apache-Maricopa-Piute	1
Pueblo	5	Redskin	1	Navajo-White	1
Laguna	5	Quechan	1	Sioux-Navajo	1
San Domingo	5	Yaqui	1	Cherokee-White	1
Omaha	4	Winnebago	1	Hopi-Apache	1
Ute	4	Pima-Maricopa	43	Zuni-Pima	1
Arickara	4	Mojave-Apache	35	Pima-Pueblo	1
Mission	3	Pima-Papago	22	Mojave-Pima	1
Seneca	3	Hopi-Maricopa	8	Pima-Seneca	1
Shoshone	3	Pima-Apache	15	Piute-Papago	1
Pawnee	3	Pima-Hopi	11	Pima-Yavapai	1

Break Down of Registration Cards (cont'd)

Tribes Represented

Pima-Choctaw	1	Pima-Yuma	1
Navajo-Mexican	1	Laguna-Papago	1
Piute-Shoshone	1	Laguna-Pueblo	1
Pima-Crow	1	Hopi-Omaha	1

Church Preference

Presbyterian	1007	Congregational	13
Not Given	401	Christian Reformed	11
Catholic	165	United Presbyterian	9
Baptist	90	Assembly of God	7
Protestant	62	Southern Baptist	7
Mormon	36	Reformed	6
Seventh Day Adventist	27	Nazarene	4
Independent	24	Mennonite	3
Lutheran	18	Christian Science	2
Methodist	15	Church of Christ	2
Episcopal	14	Church of God	2

A study of the cards shows that we have visitors to the Center from the Pacific Northwest to the midwest and all the states in between. We have had visitors from every section of the Indian country at one time or another. The local Indians make great use of the facilities at the Center, not only from the nearby reservations, but those residing within the city as well.

We still need a cooler and surely hope we do not have to go through another summer without one. We still believe an electric cooled water fountain would be a great help during the hot weather.[15]

We would like the Board members and the Churches to know that we have in operation an Equipment Fund. Any group desiring to have a project at the Center can undertake any size contribution whether large or small and it will be put in our Equipment Fund. Then when we have accumulated enough, the cooler or fountain can be purchased. There are other smaller needs, too. We will be glad to discuss them with any interested person or group.

Respectfully submitted,

CARL HIGGS, *Director*

---

[15] Has since been supplied.

APPENDIX B

To City Pastors:

We are asking your cooperation in filling this questionnaire in order that we may better determine the role the City Church is playing in the lives of Indian people living within urban areas. Frank answers to the following questions will be appreciated. Thanking you for your cooperation, I am

Yours very truly,

E. Russell Carter
Associate Dir. Indian Survey
Home Missions Council of North America
Haskell Institute, Lawrence, Kansas

1. Your Church: _____

2. Address of Church: _____

3. Membership: _____

4. Does the Church membership include any races other than native born whites? Yes _____ No _____. If so, please list (giving approximate numbers of each race):

5. Have Indians been invited to attend your Church? Yes _____ No _____

6. Number of Indians who are members: _____ Attenders: _____

7. Do you include Indians in your pastoral calling? Yes _____ No _____

8. Do Indians participate in Church activities other than corporate worship?
   Yes _____ No _____
   a. As an Indian group? _____
   b. As members of mixed groups? _____

9. In your opinion, Indians should attend
   a. Distinctly Indian Churches: _____
   b. Established Churches in which Indians are accepted as members: _____

10. Should an Indian seek membership in your Church, would the attitude of the present church body be one of
    a. Indifference? _____
    b. Friendliness? _____
    c. Hostility? _____

APPENDIX C

Please check the following:

(1) Give your *first feeling* reactions in every case.

(2) Give your reactions to each race as a *group*. Do not give your reactions to the best or the worst members that you have known, but think of the picture or stereotype that you have of the whole race.

(3) Put a cross after each race in as many of the columns as your first feelings dictate.

1. Would marry.
2. Would have as regular friends.
3. Would work beside in office or shop.
4. Would hire as laborers.
5. Would hire as overseer or administrator.
6. Would live in same neighborhood.
7. Would have merely as speaking acquaintance.
8. Would debar from my neighborhood.
9. Would debar from my city.
10. Would debar from my country.

1. Your occupation: _____

2. Your Church: _____ Address of Church: _____

3. Length of residence in City: _____

4. My contacts with Indians have been those of: (Check one or more)
   a. No contacts _____
   b. Observation only _____
   c. Neighbor _____
   d. Personal friend _____
   e. Business or professional _____
   f. Social (Clubs, organizations, etc.) _____
   g. Others _____
   _____

5. Are there Indians who are members or attenders of your Church? Yes _____ No _____

6. Should an Indian seek membership in your Church your attitude would be one of:
   a. Approval _____
   b. Disapproval _____
   c. Indifference _____

Note: Your cooperation in checking this questionnaire is greatly appreciated. Thank you.

E. Russell Carter
Associate Director Indian Survey
Home Missions Council of North America
Haskell Institute, Lawrence, Kansas

PART FOUR

A Survey of Mission Schools

Throughout the Church's work among Indians the part played by mission schools looms large. The first educational efforts directed toward the training of Indian youth were inspired by missionary motives. Hand in hand with the Bible the missionary carried the textbook. For a number of years Congress helped the mission schools through appropriations for the payment of tuition for Indian children enrolled. Presumably this practice ceased in 1896.[1] Since that time the number of Protestant Mission Schools has diminished. Yet the influence of missionary education has been beyond all proportion compared to the meagre equipment of the schools and the appropriations for their support. Through these institutions, with an *esprit de corps* and personnel peculiar to themselves, the missionaries have been able to reach the children and often through the children the adults.

Number and Location

This survey covers sixteen schools of which five may be designated as mission homes where the academic work is provided in nearby public schools or colleges. Seven of these institutions are located on reservations while nine may be considered non-reservation schools. Arizona leads with six while Oklahoma and South Dakota have three each; those reporting only one are: California, New Mexico, Washington and Wisconsin.[2]

Denominational Affiliation

The Presbyterians U.S.A. lead with four; Episcopalians and Lutherans have two each; those reporting one each are: Evangelical and Reformed, Presbyterian U.S., Disciples of Christ, Methodist, Baptist, Christian Reformed, while the Home Missions Council, now the Home Missions Division, sponsors one (Cook Christian Training School); one independent, that of the Navajo Gospel Mission, is also listed. As indicated above this is not a complete enumeration of all Protestant Mission Schools but of those from whom reports were received by October 1, 1949.

History

Some of these schools have been in operation, either as boarding or on a day basis, since 1842, the latter among the Cherokees in Oklahoma,

---

[1] See, however, Exhibit A, Federal Subsidies for Church-Operated Schools, at end of Part Four.

[2] The sixteen represent all but four in the United States; consequently a good showing. Those *not* reporting are: Goodland (Okla.), Rehoboth (N.M.), Ethete (Wyo.) and Hare Mission Home (S.D.).

established by the Moravians and taken over by the Danish Lutherans in 1892. The one most recently launched is the Navajo Bible Academy, (Arizona) opened in 1940.

Organization

The administrative authority for a majority of these schools (or homes) is vested in their respective mission boards or societies. The total staff personnel, employed on a regular or full-time basis, numbers 208, including superintendents, academic as well as teachers in religious education, boys and girls supervisors, farmers, cooks, mechanics and maintenance people.

Departments of Instruction Maintained

Eleven report some academic work from elementary through either Junior High or Senior High School; all have religious instruction classes either as part of the regular curriculum or in special week-day classes.

Membership in State or District

Of those carrying on academic instruction nine report that their courses are accredited by the state and that their staff attend state or district teachers associations.

In the case of those where no academic instruction prevails the pupils attend, as already indicated, nearby public schools or Junior colleges, bus transportation being the usual means of conveyance. Notable examples of this arrangement are: Oklahoma Presbyterian College for Girls, Durant, Okla.; Yakima Christian Mission, Wash.; St. Elizabeth's, Wakpala, S. Dak.; Cherokee Indian Mission, Oaks, Okla.; and Rosamond B. Goddard Home, North Fork, Calif.[3]

Teaching Staff

Fourteen report 113 on the teaching staff with Bacone registering 17, the Navajo Methodist Mission School, Farmington, N. M., 16, and Ganado Mission, Ariz., third in order with 14. Apparently a high standard of training is the rule rather than the exception.

Among chief problems in securing and holding personnel are: "Difficulty in getting people of superior qualifications on low salaries;" "isolation" mentioned by seven; "marriage, desire to continue own education, long hours, no automatic advance and no retirement."

The somewhat rapid turnover of staff members (some report one-fourth annually) is also reflected in the length of service. Comparatively few have served ten years or longer; the greatest turnover being among "single employees." However, one or two report a "moderate" turnover and two "none at all."

Not many Indians are employed as staff members, the reasons generally given are: "Better paying work with shorter hours available elsewhere;" "lack of qualified personnel;" however, a majority indicate an increase during the past five years.

---

[3] Closed during 1950.

Students

All but two of the schools are coeducational; the number of girls exceeding that of the boys. Two are for girls only.

Girls, 964; boys, 803; Total, 1,767.

About the only requirements are "willingness to learn" and "need for boarding school (or home) placement as well as lack of school opportunities." Quite naturally the academic or scholarship qualifications play a part in some schools depending on the respective curriculum.

The attitude of the parents may be characterized by these comments: "Most want them here because of moral and religious training children get and the close supervision they are under. Applications are nearly double that which can be accommodated." Others say: "Some are from broken homes;" "children of migrant workers;" "membership in school trebled in last twenty years;" "much greater demands;" "the parents are beginning to appreciate their responsibility towards the support of school and realize that the institution represents a temporary aspect of the church's program." A school in the Southwest adds: "More tolerance toward evangelization in school."

Records of those who have continued their education in other schools vary from "none to 99 percent;" the Navajo Methodist Mission says "23 out of 41 graduates past five years." Of five who kept records of those entering Christian work the number is 82; those going into teaching or other professions constitute a comparatively low figure.

Tribal Representation

The number of tribes represented in the 16 schools, allowing for duplicates, totals over 100; the school registering the largest number is Bacone with 39; Ganado is next with 22. While most of the students are Indians, several schools also enroll non-Indians, notably Oklahoma Presbyterian College for Girls and Cherokee Mission at Oaks, Oklahoma; at the latter "60 percent are less than one-fourth Cherokee."

Health Conditions

Seven report an "infirmary or hospital or special room" with 54 beds (not counting Ganado Mission with the Sage Memorial Hospital); either trained or practical nurses in charge. All but two specify "stated health examinations during the year;" nine have the services of a physician immediately available or on call. Very few epidemics of a serious nature have prevailed during the past two years.

The Nearest Town

Seven schools are located either in towns or near the city limits. One can boast a large city (Cook School at Phoenix). Those farthest distant are in the Navajo country. The attitude of the townspeople toward the school (including, of course, the students) is on the whole very good; 6 report "excellent;" one "enthusiastic;" two "friendly;" one says "doesn't know about us;" still another states "overcharging frequent." Apparently very little race prejudice is evident although one reports "taunting by children and segregation in town church;" another records "indifference" while still another states "reluctance in using Indian help."

Religious and Social Life

Regular worship services, Sunday School, Young People's meetings characterize the Sunday program. Three in the Southwest report "gospel teams" or "gospel walks" by students to adjacent areas. Those residing in towns encourage attendance in local churches while eight report "organized church" in connection with school. One reports "a native believers' roll." Where children are older there are student-led organizations such as youth fellowships, altar guilds, Junior Leagues, etc.

Included in social and athletic programs are: "Games with town groups and intramural; scout troops; parties at school with occasional invitations from town folks;" at Navajo Methodist Mission "the school is a member of District and State Athletic Associations; high school girls have daily gym classes; boys from 6th grade up have daily practice periods; participation in football, basketball, softball and track." All in all the social and athletic activities seem well cared for.

Tuition Fees

Tuition fees vary from "nothing" to $100 a year or $100 per semester; one says "subject is being discussed;" in a majority of cases "parents are required to provide clothing and shoes and pay for dental care;" one mission home says "county children pay board and room; charge $25.00 per year for others, scholarships for those actually in need." Except where children are too young the schools provide opportunities for partial self-support in a number of instances.

Equipment and Land

The number of buildings, including quarters for staff personnel, total 191 for the 16 schools; their state of repair: 12 say "good," one "excellent" and one "poor;" three indicate "immediate need of repair."

Nine report "farms," the acreage totaling 748; eleven report the school equipment as "good;" two "excellent;" two " poor but improving" or "constantly improving."

Budget

Under "annual budget" is usually included operation and maintenance. Fifteen reporting on this item announce the respectable sum of $603,757.70; whether this represents gross or net figures is not stated—presumably the former. One school reporting represents a "faith" mission and adds "as the Lord provides."

The proportion coming from students, such as tuition, compensation for work, etc., amounts to $104,392.14; thirteen reporting under this latter item. Nine report "scholarships available in varying amounts." Some of these are termed "work scholarships." The Cherokee Mission at Oaks, Oklahoma, announces a commendable plan: "For students graduating from high school, Dana College, Blair, Nebraska, offers $125.00 scholarship." Bacone reports no less than 14 different funds and scholarships with "a growing number provided by churches and interested individuals." At Cook School, Phoenix, Arizona, the following are available: 5 Presbyterian at $100.00; 4 Reformed Church in America at $100.00; 3 Wayne Foundation at $100.00; and one Congregational at $200.00.

Program of Advance

a. *Plans for use of institution for summer institutes, work camps, etc.*
Nine report such activities as: "D.V.B.S. Camps for underprivileged children;" "Shepherd's School for ten days at Farmington, N. M. School for about 40 illiterate boys and girls from the (Navajo) reservation;" "Conferences of various kinds." Of those not now carrying on summer activities the two following are of special interest:

"Would like summer school for remedial groups and those whose home environment is bad."

"None planned at present. Please suggest plans and program; I'm interested."

b. *Plans for Expansion.*
1. Buildings: Nine say "yes" and mention such items as "chapel, gymnasium, library," "laundry, music and science laboratory, dormitories;" "Community building and church;" "new high school being built;" "a chapel as an integral part of the Home for daily use;" "Boys dormitory to cost $30,000 with $20,000 on hand;" "Chapel and gymnasium," etc.

2. Increase of enrollment: One reports "a 30% increase." Four say "no;" another "Can't be done unless income is increased;" one says "debatable;" five say "yes," indicating "15 percent to 50 percent."

c. *What about the future of these schools?*
All but one offer helpful comments under this important heading and since they come from the "grass roots" a number are being cited herewith:

From California: "Possibly 5 years; California Welfare Agencies are assisting many needy families; improved roads doing away with isolated areas."

From Wisconsin: "In earlier years the most promising children were desired. Now stable families send children to public schools; at present children come mostly from broken or otherwise insecure or inadequate homes. Many are referred to the school by social workers and child welfare agencies. There would be no need for the school if earlier policy had been maintained. Under present policy need may continue indefinitely."

From the Southwest: "As long as boarding schools (Government) are needed this school will be needed. If the time comes when sufficient public schools will be provided for Navajo youth, then our school might be turned into a Christian home for public school students;" "Will continue as means of evangelization and follow-up of converts."

From the Dakotas: "For ten years; since it will take at least that long for any Federal Government program to guide the Indians into true citizenship which may, in turn, affect the sort of institution which will best serve the people."

From Washington: "On the present basis it should not be continued. Plan to turn it into a community center."

From Oklahoma: "Indefinite: it now has state backing and draws students from a definite territory besides Indian children (orphaned or dependent) from a larger area." Another states its case as follows: "First two years should be eliminated; college courses should be expanded; more terminal courses should be offered."

76

EXHIBIT A

Federal Subsidies for Church-Operated Schools

Repeatedly, in the past, the Indian Committee of the Home Missions Council has called attention to the un-American practice of these subsidies. In fact, at the very first interdenominational Conference of Christian Workers among Indians, held at Wichita, Kansas, September 24-26, 1919, appropriate action was taken.

A comparatively recent statement throwing light on the present day status of these schools is that found in the Study of Indian Wardship issued by the Indian Committee of the Home Missions Council in 1943 (p. 24-25).

> "In 1897, Congress declared it to be the policy of the government to make no appropriation for the education of Indian children in any school maintained by a religious sect. The matter was carried to the Supreme Court of the United States and in 1908 a decision was rendered (Quick Bear v. Leupp, 210 U. S. 50) that this prohibition did not apply to treaty and trust funds belonging to an Indian tribe. Thereafter, a few schools were maintained out of such funds at the request of the Indians themselves. Gratuity funds, however, were not used for sectarian schools, and the intent of the Congress was further emphasized by the enactment in 1917 of a law providing that 'no appropriation out of the Treasury of the United States, should be used, for the education of Indian children in any sectarian school'."

Under the title "Subsistence in Mission Schools" a recent government publication[4] confirms the present arrangement in the following language:

> "The Indian Service also contracts with nine mission schools for the education of 1,423 children. Six of these are Catholic schools. Three are Protestant. The amount requested for this purpose for 1948 was $185,500."

Furthermore, in the report on the Interior Department appropriation Bill, 1948 (80th Congress, 1st Session, House of Representatives, Report No. 279), appears the following item (p. 16):

> "The attention of the committee was called to the need *for increased funds* (italics ours) for the operation and maintenance of mission schools. A total of $185,500, the budget estimate, is recommended for this purpose."

Since official action has already been taken by the former Council to work for the speedy abolition of all subsidies out of federal or tribal funds for the support of sectarian schools, it is urged that the appropriate Committee of Home Missions Division of the National Council of the Churches of Christ in the U. S. A. take definite steps to appear before the present session of Congress through the appropriate Committees to implement this action.

---

4 "Indian Education" No. 153, Sept. 15, 1947, p. 2.

PART FIVE

A Survey of Activities of Religious Work Directors in Government Indian Schools

During 1949 a survey was conducted to determine the general economic, social, educational and spiritual conditions of the American Indians. As a part of this general survey an appropriate schedule was submitted to the Religious Work Directors working under the Home Missions Council of North America in the larger Government Indian Boarding Schools, or, as in one case, state schools where there is a sizeable number of Indian students.

The Schools Reporting

Schedules were returned from the following schools: Sherman Institute, Riverside, California; Phoenix Indian School, Phoenix, Arizona; Eastern A. and M. College, Wilburton, Oklahoma; Chemawa Indian School, Chemawa, Oregon; Chilocco Indian School, Chilocco, Oklahoma; Albuquerque Indian School, Albuquerque, New Mexico; Carson Indian School, Stewart, Nevada; Flandreau Indian School, Flandreau, South Dakota; and Haskell Institute, Lawrence, Kansas.[1]

Digest of Returns

I. GENERAL EDUCATIONAL PROGRAM

1. Age Groups Represented

A wide age range is noted in most of the schools with Haskell Institute reporting the greatest difference, 13 to 33 years. This is due largely to the extended post-graduate work offered there. Four of the nine schools include elementary instruction and include grades 1 to 12. The remaining five schools include the high school and post-high school or Junior College age groups.

a. "Problem" children

A wide variation is noted in the number of "problem" children. Replies range from "very few—perhaps 3 or 4," to "total enrollment problem children." In comparison with the reports submitted in 1941-42, fewer "problem" children are listed.

---

[1] Carson was included through the cooperation of the Woman's American Baptist Home Missions Society and the work there is interdenominational in character. Eastern A. and M. College, although not a government Indian school, includes a significant number of Indians in its enrollment and because of that fact the Home Missions Council maintains a Religious Director there.
See Appendices A and B for data on Intermountain Indian School and Jones Academy.

b. A majority of the schools reported 50% of the students were either full of half orphans.

c. Eight of the nine schools include Special or Veteran students. The one exception is Chemawa. Eastern A. and M. reports 130 Veterans and Haskell 73.

2. Tribes Represented

Sherman	1—Navajo, with 2 or 3 exceptions[2]
Phoenix	23—Navajo, Papago, Pima being largest in numbers
Eastern	7—Choctaw, Cherokee and Creek the largest in number
Chemawa	—"Northwest tribes and Navajos."
Albuquerque	8—"Apache and Navajo"
Chilocco	23—Creek, Seminole, Shawnee and Navajo leading in numbers
Carson	—"About 25 from entire West"
Flandreau	18—"Chippewa and Sioux predominate"
Haskell	72—"Creek, Choctaw, Sioux and Chippewa in greater numbers. Students come from 30 states and Alaska"

3. States Represented

Sherman	—"Mostly from Arizona and New Mexico"
Phoenix	—"Arizona, New Mexico, Utah, Nevada and California"
Eastern	—"Oklahoma, Arkansas, Texas, Kansas, Iowa, Arizona and California"
Chemawa	—"Montana, Idaho, Washington, Alaska, Oregon, California, Arizona and New Mexico"
Albuquerque	—"New Mexico and Arizona"
Chilocco	—"About 15 states—Oklahoma, Kansas, Mississippi, Texas, New Mexico and Arizona leading in numbers"
Carson	—"California, Utah, Nevada, Idaho, Oregon, Arizona and New Mexico"
Flandreau	—"Nine states—South Dakota, North Dakota, Montana and Wyoming leading in numbers"
Haskell	—"Thirty states and Alaska. Most of them come from the Plains states with Oklahoma leading in numbers"

4. Degree of Indian Blood

Wide variation is noted in the schools reporting. Five report a large percent of "full bloods." The remaining four vary from "1/64 to full" blood. It should be noted those schools reporting near 100% full blood enrollment, namely Sherman, Albuquerque and Phoenix, are those schools drawing students from less assimilated areas, while the others draw from those areas in which is to be found a higher degree of assimilation.

Sherman	—"All but 2 full blood"[3]
Eastern	—"1/64 to full blood"
Phoenix	—"717 out of 755 full blood"

[2] At present over 100 Papago children are enrolled.

Chemawa	—"265 full blood, 43 are ¾, 101 are ½"
Albuquerque	—"100% are full blood"—very doubtful![3]
Chilocco	—"½ to full"
Carson	—"¼ to full"
Flandreau	—"¼ to full"
Haskell	—"327 are full blood. Remaining 500 are ¾ or less. Only 2 are less than ¼"

5. Cultural Backgrounds of Students

An interesting comparison might be made of the cultural backgrounds and the degree of Indian blood. Those schools reporting near 100% full blood describe the cultural backgrounds in such terms as "Navajo culture", "very primitive", "Indian culture", and "backwoods culture", while those reflecting a higher degree of mixture describe the cultural background as "small town, farms, and 'hill-billy' homes", "all degrees from primitive to ultra-modern urban", "some from the best cultural surroundings, but many from the worst". "Broken or unsatisfactory homes are numerous."

6. Vocational Emphasis

A strong vocational emphasis is to be found in all the schools, with those including the elementary students giving some such training in the 7th grade.

7. Academic Standards

The schools vary rather widely in their emphasis upon academic work. Those schools including large Navajo enrollments have had difficulty in meeting State academic requirements. Sherman, Phoenix and Albuquerque report a modified system in which certain grades are accredited, but the special Navajo program is not. Chilocco reports "a strong vocational emphasis but moderate academic emphasis". Haskell and Flandreau report both schools are fully accredited; Flandreau by the Department of Education, State of South Dakota, and Haskell by the North Central High School Association with its credits being accepted by all colleges.

8. General Objectives

The objectives of all schools reporting could well be stated as follows: "To enable young Indian men and women in their problems of personal adjustment to the white man's world, in their personal development, to become prepared to earn a living and to function as citizens of the nation."

II. RELIGIOUS CENSUS

School	No. Catholics	No. Protestants	Denominations	No.
Sherman	196	364	Christian Reformed	40
			Presbyterian	118
			Independent	24
			Methodist	8
			Episcopal	7
			Baptist	3
			Nazarene	2
			Latter Day Saints	2
			Unknown	6
Phoenix	"2/3 Protestant — 1/3 Catholic — 25 Mormons"			

[3] The degree of blood is presumably listed on enrollment blanks but even so may be far from accurate.

Eastern A. & M.	12	378	Baptist	170
			Methodist	41
			Disciples	23
			Church of Christ	16
			Presbyterian	14
			Nazarene	4
			Assembly of God	1
			No Preference	109
Chemawa	"About equally divided between Protestant and Catholic"			
Albuquerque	318	222	Baptists[4]	25
			Presbyterian	32
			Mormon	7
			Nazarene	4
			Episcopal	11
			Christian Reformed	6
			Lutheran	2
			Methodist	3
			No Preference	65
Chilocco[4a]	17	426	Baptist	85
			Methodist	35
			Presbyterian	7
			Friends	1
			Assembly of God	1
			Disciples	1
			Church of Christ	1
			"Protestant"	4
			No Preference	191
Carson	100	610	Presbyterian[4b]	65
			Methodist[4b]	65
			Baptists[4b]	65
			Episcopal[4b]	65
			Misc. sects	50
			No Preference	300
Flandreau	221	190	Episcopal	94
			Presbyterian	59
			Methodist	11
			Lutheran	8
			Reformed in America	3
			Baptist	2
			Pentecostal	2
			Evangelical and Reformed	2
			Alliance—Christian and Unity	2
			Latter Day Saints	2
			No Church	2
			Do not know	3

[4] "List is incomplete as furnished by school authorities: Baptists should have 60; the Nazarenes about the same, while the Christian Reformed group is much larger than indicated."

[4a] "Out of 343 regularly enrolled high school students." "No preference" group relatively large due in part to enrollment of approximately 200 Navajo students."

[4b] Estimated number.

Haskell	210	580	Baptist	260
			Methodist	110
			Presbyterian	100
			Reformed in America	7
			Congregational	4
			Episcopal	31
			Nazarene	3
			Holiness	1
			Mormon	5
			Assembly of God	1
			No Preference	53

In totaling the numbers we find the Protestants in preponderance, but Albuquerque and Flandreau report a majority of Catholics. This of course reflects the mission programs in the reservation areas. Haskell, for instance, includes a large number of Baptists because of the long missionary program carried on in Oklahoma by the Southern Baptists as well as American Baptists. It should also be noted that with few exceptions the "no preference" listings are comparatively few and not as many as formerly; also that there are none listed as "peyote Church", "Shakers", or "Indian Religion."

III. THE PROGRAM OF RELIGIOUS WORK DIRECTORS

The statement of purpose submitted from Chemawa serves as a good summary of all statements submitted: "Our aim is to give every student training in the basic Christian beliefs through study and activities, leading to an acceptance of Jesus Christ as Saviour. Also to prepare each student as a leader in his home community."

Each Director has developed his own program to accomplish this end. It will be noted later that, although very similar in purpose, no two programs are alike.

1. Length of Service and Experience of the Directors

The length of service of all the full-time workers has been comparatively long—ranging from four years to thirty years. One part-time worker has been at Chilocco one year. In many instances the workers have had many years of missionary or teaching experience before coming to their present positions. Veva Wight of Sherman leads the group in years of service, having been there 30 years. Next in order is Haskell, 12½ years, Flandreau, 12 years, Carson, 10 years.

2. Academic Training of the Directors

Of the ten Directors, nine have had a full four year college training, and one reports two years of College training. Of the ten, six are Seminary trained and one just entering. One has a Masters degree in Sociology in addition to an A. B. degree in Religion, one reports some work done toward a Masters degree, two have had training in Schools of Social Work, several reporting short courses in Bible Institutes, summer schools, conferences, etc.

3. The Director's Conception of His Task in View of No. 1

A good summary of the task as seen by the Religious Work Directors was stated by the Director at Flandreau: "To be a friend and a guide—teaching the word of God and exemplifying the ideals of Christian living."

Another Director states his conception of the task as follows: "To enable the student to correlate the religious principles as expressed by Christ to the problems and experiences of his workaday world; to enable him to seek his place as a producing citizen and to conduct himself as a Christian both on and off the campus."

4. Program of Religious Activities On and Off the Campus

In some respects there appears to be strong similarity with respect to programs. All but one of the Directors report they conduct either a Church Service or Chapel Worship on the campus. The one exception is where the school is so close to a town where students may attend services.

All but two report they have either a Sunday School or week-day instruction on the campus.

There is a general practice of conducting denominational group meetings on the campus through the cooperation of the denominational representatives of nearby communities, and all schools have Youth Fellowship Groups such as Student Christian Associations, United Christian Youth Fellowships, etc.

All Directors are active in planning special observances of Easter, Christmas, Thanksgiving and other religious holidays.

All but two report some type of week-day religious instruction. An outstanding piece of work being done in this field is at Phoenix where the students from Cook Christian Training School conduct 25 classes each Thursday evening.[4]

The majority of Directors are active in neighboring churches when opportunity allows. Due to the fact some of the schools are rather far removed from populous areas, these opportunities are rare. However, all report occasional appointments in churches, either to preach, teach or otherwise participate. Two report rather frequent participation.

5. Student Activities

Full participation in student life is very noticeable. All Directors report they sponsor such clubs as Hiking, Hobby, Bird Study, Weaving, Folk Dancing, etc. Seven of the nine sponsor the Y.W.C.A., and in several instances the younger girls are organized as Y-Teens. Generous use is made of staff help from the schools. About the same proportion of Directors sponsor either the Hi-Y or Y.M.C.A. programs for the boys.

Most of the Directors are either directly responsible for the Boy Scouts or are active as Troop Committeemen.

Such activities as Youth Rallies, Student Sings, Athletic events get general support. One Director has developed a Student Center, a recreational activity which is open all out-of-school hours. This same Director is a member of the Student Activities Committee which schedules all extra-curricular activities.

It is quite evident that all Directors consider personal counselling as highly important. Without exception this is done in all schools in close cooperation with the Advisory staffs of the schools. The same is true of their calling in the dormitories and hospitals.

---

[5] Now changed to Sunday evening.

Strong use is made of student leadership in all cases, there being expressed the conviction that such experience serves as excellent training for future service to the Indian people.

It has been fully recognized by all Directors that full and enthusiastic cooperation with local churches, clubs, Y.M.C.A., etc., is highly important. In the case of Sherman, for instance, there has been a long and enriching contact with the Riverside Church Federation. The same is true of Haskell where the first Religious Work Director was placed, and the years following have been a story of complete and wholehearted cooperation with the Lawrence Ministerial Alliance.

Perhaps the most noticeable aspect of all the reports has to do with the strong interdenominational emphasis being given at all points. One school reports: "We do not emphasize denominational groups. No group goes off the campus for Church." World Day of Prayer observances, student Chapel Services, Student Volunteer meetings are characteristic of such activities.

Because of geographic conditions more than any other factor, many of the Directors do not extend their programs to other Indian Schools. In two cases the Directors carry responsibility in nearby Indian Schools. The Director at Flandreau conducts some activities at Pipestone, and the Director at Eastern A. and M. assumes responsibility at Jones Academy.

From all reports the Directors seem to be rather a versatile group. Singing, directing of games and plays, hobby clubs and some folk dancing all seem to be a part of the day's work.

All of the workers have seen their opportunity and responsibility to interpret the Indian people and their own religious activities to the surrounding communities. Without exception they have spoken to denominational and interdenominational meetings, service clubs, P.-T.A. groups, public schools, etc. This interpretation has been furthered by general participation in ministerial associations, State Councils of Churches, missionary conferences, both local and national in character, and interracial groups as opportunity allows. This includes, of course, the National and Regional Conferences of the Fellowship of Indian Workers.

Frequent use is made of student groups going to church and community organizations to speak and sing.

Some use is being made of radio as a medium through which to inform others of the work being done, but all Directors are making use of letter writing and the writing of articles, frequent reports to the Home Missions Council, etc.

Five report they have attended hearings relating to the Indian people and their affairs. Four report their desire to do so should the opportunity come.

There is reflected a general awareness of wider fields of service. Many of the Directors state they have surveyed to some extent other fields where need exists.

6. The Future of the Indian Schools

The Religious Directors are unanimous in their opinion that Indian Schools as such should be continued only as long as they are filling a need which cannot be met by public schools. It is noted that these needs vary, and the likelihood of public schools meeting these needs vary as well. In such schools as Sherman, Phoenix, Albuquerque and Chilocco, where there are large numbers of Navajo students, it comes as no surprise to know the general opinion is that they are filling a special need and should continue to do so for some time. In another case the Director reports: "If the school were closed most of the students would be absorbed by home communities, but some would not continue their schooling."

Some schools are doing a fairly good job of keeping in contact with students after graduation, but it is generally conceded that although being of great importance, it is difficult to do and seldom done effectively. Some of the Directors have developed a fairly effective service through personal correspondence and summer visitation to reservation areas, and at least three Directors are doing effective work though Daily Vacation Bible Schools.

There is unanimous approval and support given to "get-togethers" and conferences, both local, Regional and National. All Directors have given active and effective support to the National Fellowship of Indian Workers, both nationally and regionally.

APPENDIX A

Intermountain Indian School, Brigham City, Utah

In the spring of 1949 the Bushnell Army Hospital, at Brigham City, Utah, was transferred to the Department of the Interior for use as an Indian vocational school for training Navajo children. Remodeling of already existing buildings as well as additional quarters for class rooms will make possible the enrollment of 2,000 students.

At the present time (March, 1951) 1,342 pupils are enrolled of which 663 are registered as Protestants, 530 Roman Catholics, 60 as Latter Day Saints (Mormon) while 90 express no religious preference.

The report of the acting religious work director indicates that Sunday activities include worship services both morning and evening with an average attendance of 548 for the morning and 443 in the evening; the choir has 53 enrolled. Week-day activities include teachers' meetings on Thursday afternoon, followed by classes in religious instruction; 23 classes have already been organized with more in prospect. Pupils are grouped according to age and school levels. Nearby Protestant churches furnish a majority of the leaders while the local church cooperates wholeheartedly. An Advisory Committee, consisting of nine laymen and ministers, has been organized.

Intermountain School unquestionably presents a growing challenge to Protestant Christianity on a cooperative basis where more Navajo youth can be reached in a concentrated area than at any point on the entire Navajo reservation.

APPENDIX B

Brief Report on Jones Academy, Hartshorne, Oklahoma

Jones has dropped grades one and two and has added the ninth grade instead[6]. Enrollment is 165. No accurate record is available in the matter of church preferences (50-60% are Baptist-Southern Convention; 20% Methodist; 15% Presbyterian; one per cent Roman Catholic; 15% Nazarene, Assembly of God or 'no preference').

Tribes: Choctaw, Chickasaw, Cherokee, Seminole, Creek and Osage. States represented: Oklahoma and California. Degree of blood: one fourth to full-blood; ages, 8-18; number of orphans and half-orphans proportionately high. All students, however, come from broken homes, under-privileged circumstances, etc., or are institutional cases.

Regular Sunday School classes are held while Sunday evening assembly services are also conducted. Some of the ministers from near-by Hartshorne assist in these services while the religious work director from Wilburton, Eastern Oklahoma A & M College, supervises the program of religious activities.

[6] Lower grades restored (1951); only boys enrolled at Jones.

PART SIX

EXHIBIT A

Protestant Missions to Indians in U.S.A. Listed by Regions of the National Fellowship of Indian Workers

I. Eastern Regional Area

State	Denomination or Agency	Tribe or Tribes	Location
Maine	American Baptist (Under State Convention)	Penobscot	Indian Island
Massachusetts	American Baptist (Under State Convention)	Unknown	Marshpee and Gay-head
New York	American Baptist (under State and National)	Seneca, Tuscarora, Cayuga, Oneida	Tonawanda, Catta-raugus, Sanborn, Red House
	Episcopal	Seneca, Onondaga	Irving, Nedrow
	Friends	Allegany, Seneca	Quaker Bridge
	Methodist	Mohawk, Onondaga, Seneca	Hogansburg, Nedrow, Versailles
	Free Methodist (Under local church)	Allegany, Seneca	Salamanca
	Wesleyan Methodist	Onondaga	Nedrow
	Presbyterian U. S. A. (under State Synod)	Seneca, Shinnecock	Akron, Iroquois, Salamanca, South-ampton, L. I.,
		Mohawk	Brooklyn
Pennsylvania	Presbyterian U. S. A.	Seneca	Oil Springs Res.
Michigan	Methodist (largely under Dist. Conf.)	Chippewa, Ottawa	Burnips, Copemish, Wayland, Northport, Athens, Petoskey, Mt. Pleasant, Her-mansville, Mikado, Sault Ste. Marie, L'Anse
	Presbyterian U. S. A. (State Synod)	Chippewa	Omena
	Ev. Mission Covenant of N. A. (under District Conf.)	Chippewa	Wilson, Hannahville
North Carolina	Methodist	Cherokees Croatans	Cherokee, Pembroke (Robeson Co.)
	Southern Baptist	Cherokees	Cherokee
Alabama	Southern Baptist	Creek or Alabama	Calvert, McIntosh
Florida	Southern Baptist (under Okla. Creek-Seminole Association)	Seminole	Dania
	Episcopal (under state and local auspices)	Seminole	Everglades

II. Plains Regional Area

State	Denomination or Agency	Tribe or Tribes	Location
Wisconsin	Assembly of God (Pentecostal)	Chippewa Stockbridge	LacCourte Oreille Res., Gresham
	Christian and Missionary Alliance	Menominee, Winnebago, Oneida	Chilton, Phlox
	American Baptist (State Convention)	Winnebago	Wisconsin Dells near Baraboo
	Lutheran, Jt. Synod of Wisconsin and other states	Menominee, Stockbridge, Oneida	Red Springs, Oneida
	Lutheran, Evangelical	Oneida, Winnebago	Wittenberg
	Lutheran, American (Eielsen Synod)	Potawatomi	Carter
	Methodist	Oneida Chippewa	Odanah, West Depere
	Presbyterian U. S. A. (under State Synod)	Chippewa, Stockbridge, Menominee	Lac du Flambeau, Stone Lake, Gresham
	Episcopal	Oneida	Oneida
	Evangelical & Reformed	Winnebago, Oneida	Neillsville, (Mission School) Black River Falls
	Potawatomie Missionary Society, Independent	Potawatomi	Soperton near Stone Lake
	Ev. Mission Covenant of N. A. (under Dist. Conf.)	Chippewa Potawatomi	Stone Lake and Mole Lake near Crandon
	Church of Christ (Independent)	Oneida	Oneida
	Seventh Day Adventist	Oneida	Oneida
Minnesota	Assembly of God (Pentecostal)	Chippewa	Red Lake Res.
	Christian and Missionary Alliance	Chippewa	Onigum, White Earth, Cass Lake, Bena, Maytahwaush, Squaw Point, Inger, Vineland
	Covenant, Ev. Mission of N. A. (under Dist. Conf.)	Chippewa	Warroad, Roseau
Minnesota	Episcopal	Chippewa, Sioux	Red Lake, Redby, Cass Lake, White Earth, Leech Lake, Bena, Round Lake, Ponsford, Maytahwaush, Morton, Granite Falls Prairie Island, Pipestone
	Methodist	Chippewa	Nett Lake, Pine Bend
	Presbyterian U. S. A.	Sioux	Granite Falls
	Home Missions Council (Now under Division of Home Missions, National Council of Churches)	Chippewa, etc.	U. S. Indian School, Pipestone
Iowa	United Presbyterian	Sac and Fox	Tama
	Open Bible Church (Independent)	Sac and Fox	Tama
North Dakota	Assembly of God (Pentecostal)	Chippewa, Sioux	Turtle Mt. Res., Standing Rock
	Christian and Missionary Alliance	Chippewa, Cree, Sioux	Turtle Mt. Res., Ft. Totten (Devil's Lake)

State	Denomination or Agency	Tribe or Tribes	Location
	Congregational Christian	Arickara, Gros Ventre, Mandan, Sioux	Ft. Berthold Res. Cannon Ball, (Standing Rock Res.)
	Episcopal	Arickara, Chippewa, Sioux (Cree)	Nishu, (Ft. Berthold Res.), Dunseith, Oberon, Cannon Ball (Standing Rock Res.)
	Presbyterian U. S. A.	Sioux	Ft. Totten
	Seventh Day Adventist	Sioux	Ft. Yates (Standing Rock Res.)
	Home Missions Council of N. A.	Chippewa and Sioux, etc.	Wahpeton, N. D., U. S. Indian School
South Dakota	Assembly of God (Pentecostal)	Sioux	Yankton Res. Greenwood
	Christian and Missionary Alliance	Sioux	Fort Thompson Lower Brule
	Church of God	Sioux	Pine Ridge Res.
	Congregational Christian	Sioux	Standing Rock Res., Cheyenne River Res. Rosebud Res.
	Episcopal	Sioux	Sisseton Res., Standing Rock, Cheyenne River, Crow Creek, Lower Brule, Yankton Res., Pine Ridge, Rosebud, Flandreau, Rapid City, Pierre, Springfield, Wakpala (St. Mary's and St. Elizabeth's Mission Schools, also Hare School)
	Presbyterian U. S. A.	Sioux	Sisseton Res., Crow Creek, Pine Ridge, Yankton Res., Flandreau
	Seventh Day Adventist	Sioux	Pine Ridge Res. Red Shirt Table
	Wesleyan Methodist	Sioux	Rapid City Hot Springs
	Home Missions Council of N. A.	Sioux, Chippewa, etc.	Flandreau Indian School and Rapid City (Urban Center)
Nebraska	Assembly of God (Pentecostal)	Winnebago, Omaha	Winnebago
	Congregational Christian	Sioux	Niobrara (Bazille Creek), Santee
	Episcopal	Sioux, Ponca, Winnebago	Santee, Niobrara, Winnebago
	Reformed Church in America	Winnebago, Omaha	Winnebago, Macy
Wyoming	Episcopal	Arapahoe, Shoshone	Ethete, Ft. Washakie
Montana (N. E. part only)	Christian and Missionary Alliance	Assiniboine, Gros Ventre, Flathead	Hays (Ft. Belknap Res.) Arlee (Flathead Res.)
	Presbyterian U. S. A.	Sioux (Assiniboine)	Ft. Peck Res., Ft. Belknap Res.

III. Pacific Northwest Regional Area

State	Denomination or Agency	Tribe or Tribes	Location
Montana	American Baptist	Crow	Crow Agency, Lodge Grass, Pryor, Wyola
	Church of God	Crow	Crow Agency
	Lutheran, United, of America	Cree, Chippewa	Rocky Boy
	Methodist	Blackfeet	Browning, Babb, East Glacier Park
	Mennonite, General Conference	Northern Cheyenne	Lame Deer, Busby, Ashland
Idaho	Church of God	Nez Perce	Lapwai
	Episcopal	Bannock, Shoshone	Ft. Hall
	Methodist	Nez Perce	Lapwai
	Presbyterian U. S. A.	Nez Perce	Spaulding, Kamiah, Lapwai
Washington	Christian Church (Disciples of Christ)	Yakima	White Swan
	Church of God	Tulalip, Yakima	Marysville, Toppenish
	Four Square Gospel	Nisqually	Puget Sound Area
	Methodist	Nooksack, Swinomish, Yakima, Colville Res.	Sumas, LaConner, White Swan, Nespelem
	Pentecostal (Assembly of God)	Swinomish, Suquamish, Skagit, Quinault	LaConner, Port Madison, Port Gamble, Skagit, Public Domain,
	Presbyterian U. S. A.	Puyallup, Quinault, Makah, Spokane	Tacoma Center and Hospital, Neah Bay, Wellpinit, Taholah
	United Presbyterian (under State Synod)	Yakima	McKinley Mission near Toppenish
	Independent	Skokomish, Oakville, Queets, LaPush, Port Gamble	Puget Sound Area
Oregon	Church of God	Misc. Tribes of Puget Sound area	Celilo Falls, near The Dalles
	Four Square Gospel	Klamath, Grand Ronde, Siletz	Chiloquin, Siletz
	Methodist	Siletz, Klamath, Paiute, Modoc	Siletz, Chiloquin, Beatty, Williamson River
Oregon	Pentecostal (Assembly of God)	Klamath	Chiloquin
	Presbyterian U. S. A.	Umatilla	Pendleton
	United Presbyterian	Warm Springs, Paiute & Wasco	Warm Springs, Simnasho
	Home Missions Council of N. A.	Puget Sound and tribes of Washington and Oregon	U. S. Indian School Chemawa

IV. Western Regional Area

State	Denomination or Agency	Tribe or Tribes	Location
California	American Baptist	Mono	Auberry, Clovis, Urban Center Table Mountain, Dunlap Coarse Gold, Sycamore
	Four Square Gospel	Hoopa, Paiute, Yurok	Hoopa, Smith River, Round Valley

91

State	Denomination or Agency	Tribe or Tribes	Location
	Friends, Society of (Calif. Yearly Meeting)	Varied	Los Angeles Urban Center
	Episcopal	Paiute, Mission	Orleans, La Jolla
	Methodist	Paiute, Shoshone, Klamath and related tribes	Smith River, Round Valley, Covelo, Happy Camp
	Moravian	Mission	Banning
	Nazarene, Church of	Mission, Yuma, Mojave	La Jolla, Needles, Yuma
	Pentecostal (Assembly of God)	Paiute, Klamath, Hoopa, Shoshone, and others in northern California	Ft. Bidwell, Alturas, Likely, Orleans, Smith River, Eureka, Covelo, Ukiah, and Weitchpec
	Presbyterian U. S. A.	Hoopa, Mono, Paiute, Washoe, Shosbone, Mojave	Hoopa, Bishop, North Fork, Needles
	Independent	Varied	Los Angeles (two centers—one under Bible Institute)
	Home Missions Council of N. A.	Varied (mostly Navajos)	Sherman Institute, Riverside
Nevada	American Baptist	Paiute, Washoe, Shoshone	Dresslerville, Reno, Fallon, Stewart, (Indian School)
	Episcopal	Paiute, Washoe, Shoshone	Ft. McDermitt, Pyramid Lake (Nixon), Battle Mt., Carson, Moapa River, Las Vegas
	Methodist	Paiute, Shoshone	Walker River (Schurz) Yerington
	Pentecostal	Paiute, Shoshone	Reno, Elko
	Presbyterian U. S. A.	Paiute, Shoshone	Western Shoshone Res. Owyhee
Utah	Episcopal	Ute, Navajo	Uintah and Ouray Res., White Rocks, Randall, Bluff
	United Presbyterian	Navajo	Oljato (Extension of Navajo Res.)

V. Southwestern Regional Area

State	Denomination or Agency	Tribe or Tribes	Location
Arizona	Adventist, Seventh Day	Apache, Navajo, Pima, Maricopa	Camp Verde, Salt River (Clarkdale), Holbrook, Sacaton, Casa Grande, Laveen, Monument Valley,
	American Baptist	Apache, Hopi, Navajo	Middle Verde, Clarkdale, Keams Canon, Polacca, Second Mesa, Poston
	Baptist, Southern	Navajo, Pima, Papago	Flagstaff, Coolidge, Bapchule, Sells
	Episcopal	Navajo, Havasupai	Ft. Defiance, (Good Sheherd Home for Orphans) Flagstaff, Supai
	Lutheran, Jt. Synod of Wisconsin and other states	Apache	Fort Apache Res., White River, McNary, East Fork,

92

State	Denomination or Agency	Tribe or Tribes	Location
Arizona	Lutheran, Jt. Synod of Wisconsin and other states (Con't.)		Cibecue, San Carlos Res., Peridot, Bylas
	Mennonite, General Conf.	Hopi	Oraibi, Hoteville, Moencopi
	Methodist	Cocopah, Yuma	near Yuma, Ariz.
	Nazarene, Church of	Cocopah, Mojave, Maricopa, Navajos, Papago, Hopi	Somerton, Needles, Lehi Res., Parker, Poston, Winslow, Casa Grande
	Pentecostal (Assembly of God)	Apache, Pima, Mojave	San Carlos, White-river, Bylas, Sacaton, near Parker
	Presbyterian U. S. A.	Apache, Mojave, Navajo, Pima, Maricopa, Papago, Yaqui, Hopi	Ft. McDowell, Parker, Ft. Defiance, Kayenta, Chinle, Indian Wells, Tuba City, Ganado, (Mission School and Hospital) Leupp, Scottsdale, Sacaton, Bapchule, Casa Grande, Gila Bend, Sells, Ajo Phoenix and Tucson (Escuela) Mission School Blackwater Clarkdale Vah-Ki Prescott Maricopa Gila Crossing Coop Vamori Santa Rosa Darby Wells San Miguel
	Plymouth Brethren	Navajo, Pueblo, Walapai	Red Rock, Winslow, Valentine, Peach Springs
	Reformed, Christian	Navajo	Camps near Phoenix, Tez Nos Pas (on Navajo Res.)
	Independent 1. Good News Mission	Navajo	Houck
	2. Navajo Gospel Mission	Navajo	Oraibi (16 mi. north)
	3. Navajo Bible School	Navajo	Window Rock (2 mi. s. e.)
	4. Hopi Mission	Hopi	Polacca (Byron P. Adams)
	5. Hopi Mission	Hopi	Oraibi (Fred A. Johnson)
	6. San Carlos Mission	Apache	San Carlos (Walker Tonto)
	7. Mojave Mission	Mojave	Parker
	Home Missions Council of N.A.	Navajo, varied	Literacy Project, Tonalea; U. S. Indian School, Phoenix; Cook

State	Denomination or Agency	Tribe or Tribes	Location
Arizona	Mojave Mission Home Missions Council of N.A. (Con't)		Christian Training School, Phoenix; Phoenix Indian Center
New Mexico	Adventist, Seventh Day	Navajo	Thoreau (Now at Holbrook, Ariz.)
	Baptist, Southern	Navajo, Pueblo	Farmington, Gallup, Laguna, Albuquerque (Indian School and Center), Isleta, Bernalillo, Santa Fe (Indian School & Center), Canon Cito
	Episcopal	Navajo	Farmington San Juan Mission (Hospital), Fruitland, Carsons
	Methodist	Navajo	Farmington (Mission School), Fruitland, Bisti, Huerfano
	Methodist, Free	Navajo	Gallup
	Nazarene, Church of	Navajo, Pueblos	Albuquerque (Center near Indian School), Lindrith (Mission School), Pena Blanca, Gallup, Ramah
	Plymouth Brethren	Navajo	Shiprock
	Presbyterian U. S. A.	Pueblos	Seama, Casa Blanca, Jemez, Paguate
	Reformed Church in America	Jicarilla, Apache, Mescalero Apache	Dulce, Mescalero, White Tail
	Reformed, Christian	Navajo, Zuni	Rehoboth (School & Hospital), Gallup, Ft. Wingate School, Tohatchi, Toadlena, Shiprock, Farmington, Crown Point, Carisso, Red Rock, Beautiful Mountain, Nahaschitty, San Antone, Star Lake, Two Wells, Zuni (School), Black Rock
	Independent 1. Brethren in Christ	Navajo	Bloomfield, Councillor near Cuba
	2. Wycliffe School of Bible Translators	Navajo	Farmington
	Home Missions Council of N. A.	Varied	U. S. Indian School, Albuquerque
Colorado	Presbyterian U. S. A.	Navajo, Ute	Towaoc, Ignacio
	Reformed, Christian	Navajo	U. S. Indian School Ignacio

VI. Oklahoma Regional Area

State	Denomination or Agency	Tribe or Tribes	Location
Kansas	Methodist	Potawatomi	Mayetta
	Home Missions Council of N. A.	Varied	Haskell Institute, Lawrence
Oklahoma	Adventists, Seventh Day	Cherokee, Choctaw	Tahlequah, Wilburton, Vian

State	Denomination or Agency	Tribe or Tribes	Location
Oklahoma	American Baptist[1]	Comanche, Caddo, Wichita, Kiowa, Delaware, Apache, Cheyenne, Arapahoe, also those enrolled at Bacone	Walters, Deyo, Red Stone, Apache Wichita near Anadarko Elk Creek, Rainy Mt., Saddle Mt., Greenfield, Swappingback, Watonga, Kingfisher, Bacone, U. S. Indian Schools at Ft. Sill, Riverside, Concho (see map)
	Baptist, Southern	Cherokee, Creek, Seminole, Choctaw, Chickasaw, Quapaw, Seneca, Ponca, Pawnee, Otoe, Osage, Sac & Fox, Kickapoo, Potawatomie, Shawnee, Wichita, Caddo, Chilocco	50 missionaries on either half or part time; 5 general full-time missionaries; 95 churches; work at Chilocco Govt. School; also centers at Muskogee, Tulsa and Oklahoma City
	Baptist, Independent (Affiliated with Southern Baptists)	Seminole, Cherokee, Creek, Choctaw	10 or 12 among Seminoles & Creeks; others scattered in eastern Oklahoma
	Church of God	Cherokee	Park Hill
	Friends	Seneca-Cayuga, Osage, Kickapoo, Shawnee	Wyandotte, Council House, Hominy, McLoud, Shawnee (Sanitarium)
	Gospel Missionary Union	Cherokee	Eastern Oklahoma, e.g., Cher. Delaware & Adair Co.
	Lutheran, United Ev.	Cherokee	Oaks (Mission School and two centers)
	Mennonite (Gen'l. Conf.)	Cheyenne, Arapahoe,	Canton, Clinton, Weatherford; also Concho School
	Mennonite Brethren	Comanche	Postoak Ft. Sill Gov't School,
	Methodist[1]	Cherokee, Choctaw, Chickasaw, Creek, Seminole, Comanche, Kiowa, Apache, Ponca, Osage, Cheyenne Shawnee	"41 pastors, 1 Gen. Supt.; 3 Dist. Supts.; 4 women workers" 97 churches; also centers at Oklahoma City, Tulsa, Muskogee; work in gov't. schools (see map)
	Nazarene, Church of	Cheyenne, Arapahoe, Comanche, Apache, Ponca	Clinton, Colony, Apache, El Reno, Walters, Ponca City
	Pentecostal	Kiowa, Comanche, and points in eastern Oklahoma	
	Presbyterian U. S. A.[1]	Choctaw, Creek, Seminole, Cherokee	24 churches (see map)

[1] See map, p. 120.

95

State	Denomination or Agency	Tribe or Tribes	Location
	Presbyterian, Cumberland[2]	Choctaw, Cherokee	12 part-time pastors; 17 churches, mostly in eastern Oklahoma (see map)
	Presbyterian U.S.[2]	Choctaws, Chickasaws; also those at Oklahoma Presbyterian College and Goodland	13 churches (see map); also Oklahoma Presbyterian College for Girls, Durant and Goodland Orphanage, Hugo
		various tribes	Talihina Indian Hospital
	Presbyterian, Reformed	Comanche, Apache	Apache (Cache Creek Mission)
	Presbyterian, United	Cherokee; also at Wheelock Academy	Stilwell; Wheelock Academy, Millerton
	Reformed Church in America	Comanche, Apache	near Lawton; also work at Ft. Sill Indian School
	Independent	Cherokee	"Go Ye" Mission at Tahlequah; carry on some work at Sequoyah and other schools
	Independent — The National Indian Association	Cherokee	Vian, S.S. and Community Work
	Home Missions Council of N. A.	Varied	Chilocco, Jones Academy, Eastern A. & M., Wilburton, Sequoyah near Tahlequah
Texas	Presbyterian U. S.	Alabama and Coushatta	near Livingston (Polk County)
Louisiana	Congregational Christian	Coushatta	near Kinder
Mississippi	Baptist, Southern	Choctaw	4 stations near Philadelphia and Carthage
	Methodist	Choctaw	near Philadelphia

[2] See map, p. 120.

PART SIX

EXHIBIT B

Protestant Missions to Indians in United States of America

Some Overall Data

I. Boards Constituent to Home Missions Council of North America

I *Name*	*State*	*Tribe*	*Location*	*II* *Full Time*	*Part Time*	*Native*	*III* *Stations*
1. Church Ex- tension and Home Missions of the Church of God	Oklahoma South Dakota Montana Idaho Washington Washington Oregon	Cherokee Sioux Crow Nez Perce Suquamish Interracial Mixed group of Northwest Indians	Park Hill Wounded Knee Crow Agency Lapwai Tulalip Toppenish Celilo Falls	18	2	1 (f.t.)	10
2. Women's Gen- eral Missionary Society of United Presby- terian Church of North America	Oregon Oregon Iowa Oklahoma Oklahoma Arizona Utah	Wasco, Piute & Warm Spring Tenino and Wasco Mesquakie, Sac and Fox Cherokee Choctaw (Wheelock Academy) Navajo Navajo	Warm Springs Simnasho Tama Stilwell Millerton Chilchinbito Oljato	4	1	2(f.t.)	6
3a. Division of Home Missions and Church Extension of the Methodist Church[1a]	Arizona California- Nevada Central N. Y. Detroit, Mich. Genesee, N.Y. Kansas Michigan	Cocopah Yuma Digger Paiute Shoshone Onondaga Chippewa Ottawa Seneca Cayuga Pottawatomie Chippewa	Yuma Guschu Round Valley Klamath River Schurz- Yerington Onondaga Algonquin Oscoda Indian Falls Potawatomie Mt. Pleasant Northport Bradley	Total Number 27		31	dif- ferent missions

IV Schools & Spec. Projects	Church Members	V Adherents[1]	Total	VI Budget Local	Contributed by Board
	300	650	$16,500.00	$4,500.00	$12000.00
Wheelock Academy Millerton, Okla.	94	295	$10,500.00 Doesn't include work in Arizona launched in Sept. 1949	Whole budget is contributed by Soc.	Whole budget is contributed by society
	3,799[2]		$108,000.00	$34,000.00	$74,000.00

---

[1] Since the number of adherents is difficult to determine this column is frequently left blank; however, the Protestant constituency as a whole approximates 140,000.

[1a] The data as presented was received too late to be included in over-all information for the Columbus Congress, but is listed herewith.

[2] "Several not reporting; off-hand this figure should be increased by at least a thousand"

I Name	State	Tribe	Location	II Full Time	Part Time	Native	III Stations
	Minnesota	Chippewa	Nett Lake Pine Bend				
	Montana	Blackfeet (Piegan)	Piegan-Browning Piegan-Babb Piegan-Glacier Piegan-Sweet Pine				
	North Carolina	Cherokee (Croatan)	Pembroke Circuit Pembroke Parish Bethel Community Cen. Fairview First Hickory Grove Hopewell Pleasant Grove Prospect Samson Mem. Sandy Plains				
	Northern N.Y.	Mohawk	St. Regis Falls Dickinson Center				
	Oregon	Siletz Klamath Modoc Paiute	Siletz Klamath Bly Beatty				
	Pacific North-west	Nooksack	Nooksack				
	Washington	Swinomish Colville Yakima	LaConner Nespelem Cottonwood White Swan				
	Idaho	Nez Perce	Lapwai				
	West N.C.	Cherokee	Cherokee				
	West Wisconsin	Chippewa	Odanah				
	Wisconsin	Oneida	Oneida				
3b. The Methodist Mission of Oklahoma[3]	Okla.	Cherokee, Choctaw Creek, Euchee, Seminole, Shawnee Comanche, Kiowa Apache Ponca, Osage, Cheyenne; also those in urban centers.	(See map of Okla. p. 120)	45	all native (Except Gen. Supt. and three women workers)		97

[3] The Indian Mission of Oklahoma has a unique place in Methodist Indian work; aside from the General Superintendent, the Executive Secretary and two Deaconesses, all the staff are Indians, including three district Superintendents and one contract woman worker.

IV Schools & Spec. Projects	Church Members	V Adherents	Total	VI Budget Local	Contributed by Board
Urban centers; Summer Institutes; social & Community service	5,301	10,000		Budget included under 3a.	

101

I Name	State	Tribe	Location	II Full Time	Part Time	Native	III Stations
3c. Women's Division of the Board of Missions and Church Extension of the Methodist Church[1a]	New Mexico	Navajo	Farmington, N.M.	33 (Includes Mission School staff)	3	4	3
4. Women's Board of Domestic Missions, Reformed Church in America	Oklahoma	Comanches and Apaches	Lawton	4 ordained white 5 1 ordained native			
	Nebraska	Omahas	Macy	1 native assistant studying ordination			
	Nebraska	Winnebagoes	Winnebago				
	New Mexico	Jicarilla-Apache	Dulce	4 native interpreters			
	New Mexico	Mescalero-Apache and Whitetail-Apache	Mescalero				
5. Christian Reformed Board of Missions	Arizona	Navajo	Carisso and Phoenix	54	1	17	44
	New Mexico	Navajo	Crown Point Farmington Gallup, Nahaschitty, Red Rock, Rehoboth, San Antone, Shiprock, Toadlena, Tohatchi, Two Wells				
	New Mexico	Zuni	Zuni				
6. Women's American Baptist Home Missions Society	Arizona	Hopi	Polacca, Toreva	2	3		
	California	Mono	Clovis (Missionaries work at Sycamore also)	2			2
	Montana	Crow					
	Montana	Crow	Lodge Grass Wyola	2			2
	Nevada	Piute-Shoshone	Stewart	2			1 stat. 2 outsta
							3
	Oklahoma	Cheyenne Arapahoe	Watonga Kingfisher	2			2
	Oklahoma	Kiowa	Saddle Mountain Indian Mission	1			

102

IV Schools & Spec. Projects	V Church Members	Adherents	Total	VI Budget Local	Contributed by Board
Farmington: Boarding School, Grades pre-first through twelfth; 183 pupils; 209 Church Members; Average attendance 210.			$66,445.00	$14,603.00	$51,842.00
Bisti: Boarding School of 37 pupils, Grades pre-first through second; Weekly Religious service; average attendance 45					
Huerfano: Day School of 24 pupils, Grades pre-first through third. Sunday Service: average attendance 20.					
Burnham: Community Religious Service: average attendance 40; Weekly clinic by registered nurse.					
Fruitland: Religious Education Classes weekly in government school with 74 pupils in the Methodist group. Sunday afternoon service with average attendance of 20.					
Tsaya: Weekly Religious Service: average attendance of 10.					
One shelter for Indian children at Winnebago. Social and religion centers at all mission fields.	600	400		Assume all expenses except salaries of missionaries	$27100.00
Day school at Zuni, New Mexico. Boarding school at Rehoboth, New Mexico and Hospital.	716	303	$231,093.19	$3000.00	Everything else
	64 (Arizona) no organized (Calif.) church		$4,050.00	$100.00 $190.00	$4060.00
	Clovis—45 Sycamore—57 Lodge Grass—209 (Mont.) Wyola—25			Clovis $980.00 Sycamore $160.00 Lodge Grass $50.00 Wyola	$3940.00
Carson Indian School Stewart, Nev.	Stewart—100 (Nevada) Dresslerville—25 Reno—45			Stewart $450.00 Dresslerville $130.00 Reno $85.00	$3710.00
Bacone College Bacone, Okla.	Watonga—50 (Okla.) Kingfisher—30			Watonga $85.00 Kingfisher $45.00	$4080.00

[1a] The data as presented was received too late to be included in over-all information for the Columbus Congress, but is listed herewith.

I Name	State	Tribe	Location	II Full Time	Part Time	Native	III Stations
7. United Christian Missionary Society—Disciples of Christ	Washington	Yakima and affiliated tribes (14 in all)	White Swan	5			1
8. Board of National Missions, Evangelical & Reformed Church	Wisconsin	Winnebago	Niellsville, Black River Falls	3	1		3
9. American Baptist Home Mission Society	Arizona	Hopi, Navajo	Keams Canon Poston				4
		Camp Verde Apache	Verde Valley				3
	California	Mono	Near Fresno				4
	Montana	Crow	Crow Agency, Lodge Grass & Pryor				4
	Nevada	Washoe, Piute, Shoshone	Stewart, Reno, Dresslerville				3
	New York	Seneca Tuscarora	Cattaraugus, Tonawanda & Tuscarora Reservations				3
	Oklahoma	Comanche, Wichita, Caddo, Delaware, Apache Kiowa, Cheyenne & Arapahoe	Western Oklahoma	16	6	7	9
10. Board of Home Missions of the Congregational Christian Church	South Dakota North Dakota Nebraska	Sioux Arickara Gros Ventre Mandan	West River area & North West Nebraska Fort Berthold Res., No. Dakota	16	15		31
11. Presbyterian Church, U.S.— Executive Committee of Home Missions	Oklahoma Texas	Choctaw and Chickasaw Coushatta and Koasati	Southeastern Oklahoma (See map p. 120) Livingston, Texas	10	5		14

IV Schools & Spec. Projects	V Church Members	Adherents	Total	VI Budget Local	Contributed by Board
Boarding home for children attending public school; summer itinerant work at Celilo Falls, Oregon	68			$275.00 $315.00 Toward building and equipment	$2040.00
	Members formerly affiliated with church at Yakima; Mission church to be organized		$29,603.10	$14182.96	$15430.14
Mission School Coop store at Black River Falls	135	200	$59,900.00	Farm in connection supplies part.	Woman's Guild & Board of National Missions
	1724		$74,500		
Carson Indian School					
Bacone, College Bacone, Okla. Indian Schools at Riverside, Fort Sill, Concho. Latter 4 are government schools where missionaries assist in Religious Education					
	1142	4000	$26,069.00	$3469.00	$12600.00 Other— $10000.00
Oklahoma Presbyterian College for Girls, Goodland Indian Orphanage, latter has 12 tribes represented	787		$14,906.00 Note: Budget does not include Mission schools	$3986.00	$10938.00

I Name	State	Tribe	Location	II Full Time	Part Time	Native	III Stations
12. Associated Executive Committee of Friends on Indian Affairs	Oklahoma	Seneca-Cayuga, Osage, Kickapoo, Shawnee	All in Oklahoma	8	2		4
13. Department of Rural Church Work (Indian) of the Board of National Missions, Presbyterian Church, USA	South Dakota North Dakota Montana Minneapolis Idaho Nevada Colorado California California Oregon Oregon Washington Washington Oklahoma Oklahoma Oklahoma Arizona Arizona Arizona Arizona New Mexico	Sioux Assiniboine Gros Ventre — Nez Perce Shoshone Ute & Navajo Paiute, Mono Hoopa Umatilla Cayuse Makah, Spokane Quiniault Choctaw, Creek Seminole Cherokee Navajo Maricopa, Mohave Apache, Pima Papago Pueblo		20[4] 13[5] 24[6] 8	4[7] 1[8]		21 unorganized preaching stations 112 organized churches
14. Protestant Episcopal Church, Division of Domestic Missions	Arizona — Wisconsin Idaho	Navajo Havasupai Oneida Shoshone Bannock Lemhi	Ft. Defiance Supai, Canon Oneida Ft. Hall	6 1 3 1	1	1	4 1 2 1
	Minneapolis	Chippewa	Bena, Cass Lake Maytahwaush, Onigum Ponsford, Redby, Round Lake White Earth, Rice Lake	8		4	9
	Nebraska	Ponca Winnebago	Niobrara Winnebago	1			2
	Nevada	Pauites	Moapa, Res, Nixon	2			2
	New Mexico	Navajo	Farmington Carsons	2	2		2
	North Dakota	Sioux Chippewa Mandan Arickara	Ft. Totten Turtle Mt. Standing Rock Ft. Berthold	4	1		4
	New York	Onondaga Seneca	Onondaga Res. Irving	2		1	2
	South Dakota	Sioux	Cheyenne Acy. Crow Creek Lower Brule	25	48	64	97

106

IV Schools & Spec. Projects	V Church Members	Adherents	Total	VI Budget Local	Contributed by Board
Religious Education in-Seneca Indian School, Wyandotte; Services at Government Indian Sanatorium, Shawnee	150	1000			$12800.00
1 Mission School (Ariz.) 1 Clinic (Ariz.)	9 states 5114		$182,259.00	$5413.00 (for support of ministers) $14197.00 (raised by Indian churches for local Church expenditures)	$156989.00 $3450.00 (Synod) $2210.00 (Presbyteries)

1

	181 (Ariz.) Navajo	800	no data	not listed	$19,550
1	35 Havasupai	100			
Religious Education in Government Schools	697 (Wisconsin)	1000	Support comes from state & local		
	100 (Idaho)	350	Support comes from state & local		$ 4,160
Religious Education in Indian Schools	1160 (Minn.)	2000	Support comes from state & local		$ 5,000
	68 (Neb.)	200	Support comes from Diocese		
	90 (Nevada)	350	Support comes from Diocese		
	119 (N. Mexico)	350			$11,930
	245 (N. Dakota)	600			$ 4,505
	143 (New York)	250	Support comes from Diocese		
	4800 (S.Dakota)	10000			$70,760
	50 (Calif.)	100			$ 2,240
	422 (Utah)	800			$ 4,200
	265 (Wyoming)	750			$17,030

Total $139,375

San Jaun Hospital at Farmington
Religious Education in Government Schools

St. Mary's & St. Elizabeth's Hare School

[4] Of which 3 are native
[5] All of these missionaries are natives
[6] Of which 23 are natives
[7] All four are natives
[8] Native

I Name	State	Tribe	Location	II Full Time	Part Time	Native	III Stations
			Flandreau				
			Pine Ridge				
			Rosebud,				
			Santee				
			Sisseton				
			Yankton				
			Standing Rock				
	California	Karok	Orleans	1			
	Utah	Utes	White Rocks	2			
		Navajo	Utah "Strip"				3
	Wyoming	Arapahoes	Ethete				
		Shoshones	Wind River	3	1	2	3
15. Home Missions Council of North America	Arizona	All South West Tribes	Phoenix	2	3		3
			Not counting Cook School Staff				
	California	Navajo	Riverside	2			1
	New Mexico	Apache Navajos Hopi, etc.	Albuquerque	1			1
	Oklahoma	20 Tribes	Wilburton Jones Academy Talihina Chilocco Sequoyah	1	4	3	4
	Kansas	57 Tribes	Haskell Inst.	1	1		1
	South Dakota	Sioux	Flandreau	2		1	2
		Chippewa	Non-Res. Wk.				
	North Dakota	Winnebago Oneida	Wahpeton		1		1
	Minnesota	Chippewa	Pipestone		1		1
	Oregon	12 tribes	Chemawa	1			1

16. Department of Educational and Medical Work of the Board of National Missions — Presbyterian — U.S.A.[1a]

I. *Institutions*

Name	Location	Type	Tribes Represented in Student Body
Tucson Indian Training School	Southern Arizona	Boarding School Co-Ed, 114 Students	Pima Papago Apache Paiute Mono Mohave-Apache Sioux Paiute-Papago Mohave

---

[1a] The data as presented was received too late to be included in over-all information for the Columbus Congress, but is listed herewith.

Schools & Spec. Projects	Church Members	Adherents	Total	Budget Local	Contributed by Board
Religious Education in Government Schools St. Michael's Mission School					
Linguistics, Cook Training School, Phoenix	No church membership listed				$45,167.83 (including part of budget Cook Christian Training School)
Indian Center Religious Edu. ditto					
ditto ditto Hospital Minis. Religious Edu.					
ditto					
Urban center					
Religious Edu. Religious Edu. Religious Edu.					

II. *Number of Missionaries*

States Repre. in Student Body

Arizona

California
South Dakota
Nevada

Full time, commissioned 85
Full time, maintenance 23

Note: Records do not distinguish between native and non-native,
so above figures include both.

III. Stations — 5
See I and add following outstation to Ganado Mission:
Cornfields Community Center
Tselani Community Center

IV. All projects listed above

V. Student Church Membership — 240

109

I. Institutions

Name	Location	Type	Tribes Represented in Student Body
			Navajo
			Pima-Papago
			Hopi-Maricopa
			Pima-Yavapai
			Chemehuevi
			Papago-Maya
			Maricopa
			Yuma
			Navajo-Hopi
			Hopi-Pima-Hoopa
			Pima-Navajo
			Shoshone
			Pima-Hopi
			Papaga-Navajo
			Tonto-Apache
			Washoe-Pittriver
			Yaqui
Ganado Mission	Northern Arizona	Boarding School Co-ed, 167 Students Community Stations	Navajo Hopi Laguna Hopi-Navajo Hopi-Tewa Acoma-Laguna Tule Walapai Choctaw Creek Hopi-Papago Navajo-Papago Tewa Washoe Cherokee-Navajo Hopi-Ute Ute Papago-Maya Laguna-San Juan Mohave-Apache
Ganado Mission	Northern Arizona	Hospital School of Nursing 28 Students	Navajo Hopi Shoshone Laguna Paiute Eskimo Thlinget Mission Sandia Taos Papago
Rosamond B. Goddard[9]	California	Home 47 Children	Mono Chuchonsi Paiute Wintun Miwak Klamath Mission Hoopa

[9] Closed Sept. 1950

VI. Budgets — 1949

	Total Gross Appropriation excluding Salaries	Raised on Field Tuition, Fees, etc.
Tucson	$27,000	$4,200
Ganado—Mission	53,000	7,300
Hospital	65,000	23,000
R. B. Goddard Home	10,000	3,300

Arizona
New Mexico
Nevada
California
Oklahoma
Utah
Colorado

New Mexico
Arizona
California
Nevada
Colorado
Alaska

Arizona
Oregon
California

2. Non-Constituent or Non-Sectarian

I Name	State	Tribe	Location	II Full Time	Part Time Native	III Stations
1. Mennonite Brethren, Church of North America	Oklahoma	Comanche		6	2	2
2. Home Missions Board, Southern Baptist Convention	Oklahoma	All tribes except Cheyenne, Arapahoe, Kiowa, Comanche and Apache (No data available on work in other states)		50 either ½ or part-time. A general missionary among Cherokees, 1 among the Creeks, and 1 among Choctaws and Chickasaws with 2 assistants. A field worker among the women for the whole state. A missionary at Chilocco Indian School; and others are missionaries or pastors of Indian churches.		
3. General Missionary Board of Free Methodist Church	New Mexico	Navajos	Gallup	1 Missionary		
4. General Council Assemblies of God	Washington	Quillayute, Makah, Elwha, Spokane-Colville, Skokomish Reservations.		50 workers		
	Idaho	Bannocks				
	Montana	Blackfeet and Assiniboines				
	North Dakota	Sioux				
	Minnesota	Chippewa				
	Wisconsin	Chippewas and Stockbridge				
	Nebraska	Winnebago Omaha				
	Arizona	Apache Pima				
	New Mexico	Navajo				
	Oregon	Klamath Reservation and Warm Springs Reservation				
5. Christian and Missionary Alliance	Minnesota Wisconsin	Chippewa Oneida Menominee Winnebago		36	2 (t.f.)	15
	North Dakota	Chippewa				

IV Schools & Spec. Projects	Church Members	V Adherents	Total	VI Budget Local	Contributed by Board
I	150		350 8—$10,000.00		
Do not operate day schools or hospitals	7,500	Information not available			
	none		$700 a year		
none	Data not available			Most districts match amount supplied by National	$15,600.00
Mo-Kah-Um Indian Bible School	12 churches	745 estimated	$18,700.00	Not much	$11,000.00

I Name	State	Tribe	Location	II Full Time	Part Time	Native	III Stations
	Montana	Arikara Gros Ventre Mandan Cree Flathead Blackfeet Chippewa, Cree, Gros Ventre Assiniboine Sioux					
	South Dakota	Sioux					
6. Lutheran Synod of Wisconsin and other states	Arizona	Apache	San Carlos Ft. Apache	9 8 interpreters		3 teachers	8 stat. 12 outst. — 20
7. Plymouth Brethren: not a denomination: have no board officials; no statistics kept, Faith mission	Arizona New Mexico Arizona	Havasupai Navajos Pueblo Apaches and Navajo	Valentine Emmanuel West of Shiprock New Mexico	9			3
8. North America Indian District of the Church of the Nazarene	California Arizona New Mexico Oklahoma Montana Michigan	Cocopahs, Dieguinos, Mission Indians, Mojaves, Quechans, Chemehuevis, Navajos, Pueblos, Maricopas, Papagos, Poncas, Cheyennes, Araphoes, and Comanche		46		9 interpreters	20 st. 4 outst. — 24
9. Wesleyan Methodist Church of America, Department of Home Missions	New York South Dakota Ontario	Onondaga Sioux St. Regis	Nedrow Hot Springs & Rapid City Cornwall Island, Cornwall, Ontario	10	1	2	4
10. Navajo Gospel Mission, Inc., Faith Mission	Arizona	Navajo	District No. 4— No. of Oraibi, Arizona	13		6	4
11. National Indian Association (nonsectarian)	Oklahoma	Cherokee	Vian, Oklahoma	1			3
12. Cumberland Presbyterian Church	Oklahoma	Choctaw and Cherokee	Choctaws in S.E. Oklahoma; Cherokee with whites in North East Oklahoma (See map p. 120)	1	16	17	17

114

IV Schools & Spec. Projects	Church Members	V Adherents	Total	VI Budget Local	Contributed by Board
4 and a nursery Going to build on other school Have one boarding school	11 churches	3,000	$103,235.03		All by National
Indian Training School at Landrith	616		$65,000.00	$12,936.00	
David Brainerd Indian Training School near Hot Springs, South Dakota	38 members at Onondaga; others not organized		(Note: Does not include the Rapid City South Dakota Mission and the Brainerd School near Hot Springs, South Dakota. No budget figures submitted.)		
Navajo Bible Academy	36	1,000	No amount indicated: "We work as the Lord provides the means."		
Religious instruction in public schools and Sunday School work	none	300	$2,635.85		
none	488	1,200	$3,069.00	$2,769.00	$3,000.00

I				II		III
Name	State	Tribe	Location	Full Time	Part Time	Native Stations
13. Reformed Presbyterian Church	Oklahoma	Comanche, Kiowa and Apache	West of Apache, Oklahoma	1		1
14. Society for Propagating Gospel among Indians and Others in North America		All tribes			1	

3. Independent (Southwest)

I	II	III
Mission Stations and Outstations	Visitations and Camp Work	Govt. Boarding or Day School
A. Independent Hopi Mission No outstations	At old and new Oraibi, Hopi villages in Arizona	none
B. Good News Mission Hauck, Arizona	Camp work done in this area	
Reg. weekly services at 1) Lupton 2) Hauck 3) Sanders noonday classes held for Navajo school children		1 day school at Hauck Station.
C. Independent Hopi Mission Polacca, Arizona	5 Hopi villages	none
D. Brethren in Christ Mission % Blanco Trading Post, Bloomfield, New Mexico. 1 station near Blanco Trading Post among Navajos. No outstations.	Visitation in Government District 19 and surrounding area	1 Government school. Do no religious instruction there

IV Schools & Spec. Projects	Church Members	V Adherents	Total	VI Budget Local	Contributed by Board
none at present	60	300	$2,500.00		
Cooperates with Home Missions Council	none		$2,500.00		All

IV Location of Mission Schools, Hospitals, etc.	V Unmet Needs	VI New Work
Oraibi, Arizona	Need for Indians to support their own ministers and missionaries	Indian Bible conference for our South West Indians, Prescott, Arizona
	We believe a dispensary or some medical help would be extremely beneficial. We carry on a limited dispensary but a well equipped unit would serve.	None — further than what we are able to do.
none	none	More responsibilities in taking charge of activities and services.
Expect to have a boarding school, community center, and clinic eventually.	There is urgent need for a hospital in the district though it seems doubtful if any of the groups working here are able (if desirous) of undertaking such a project.	Educational and medical work, as well as an extensive evangelistic program, all of which is in a sense new, as it is less than 3 years old; have only been located at present location for a year.

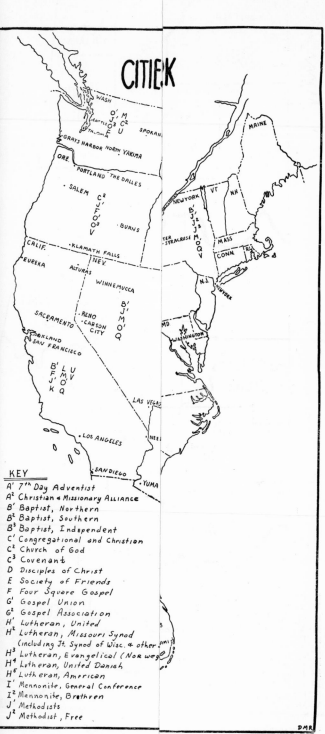

CITIES

KEY
A¹ 7ᵗʰ Day Adventist
A² Christian & Missionary Alliance
B¹ Baptist, Northern
B² Baptist, Southern
B³ Baptist, Independent
C¹ Congregational and Christian
C² Church of God
C³ Covenant
D Disciples of Christ
E Society of Friends
F Four Square Gospel
G¹ Gospel Union
G² Gospel Association
H¹ Lutheran, United
H² Lutheran, Missouri Synod (including Jt. Synod of Wisc. & other
H³ Lutheran, Evangelical (Norweg.
H⁴ Lutheran, United Danish
H⁵ Lutheran, American
I¹ Mennonite, General Conference
I² Mennonite, Brethren
J¹ Methodists
J² Methodist, Free

Indian Missionary wor
Protestant Ind

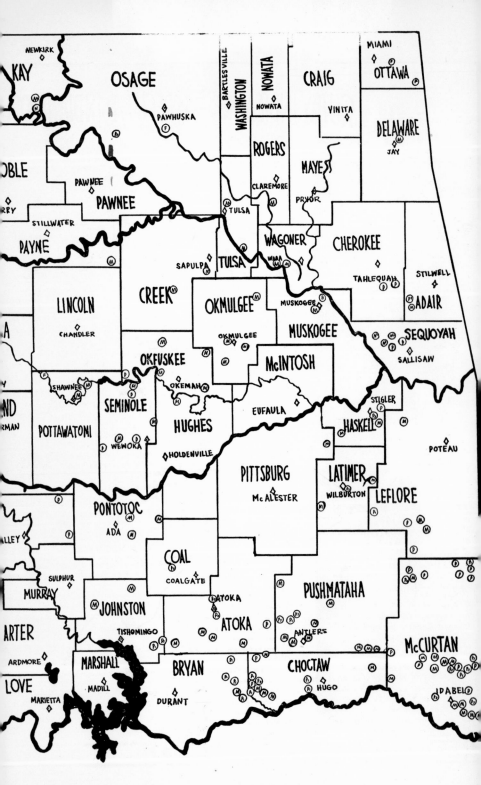

k as carried on by agencies cooperating in the
lian Council of Oklahoma

DATE DUE

DEC 0 7 1992			
FEB 1 8 1993			
APR 0 9 1993			
NOV 0 7 1994			
nov 1 3 1997			
OCT 2 8 2003			
NOV 2 6 2009			
GAYLORD			PRINTED IN U.S.A.